THE ART OF DRAWN WORK
by
The Butterick Publishing Company

Working with a woven fabric to produce openwork was the precursor of true lace, where openwork is created without any base fabric. There are three basic techniques which developed simultaneously for manipulating a woven fabric to produce openwork designs. Referred to as *CUT WORK, PULL WORK* and *DRAWN WORK*, all three remain an essential part of today's needlework vocabulary.

In CUT WORK, the threads are simply cut out in geometric or free form shapes depending on the specific type of cut work. Hardanger and Reticella are names associated with designs based on geometric openings while Richelieu is the name assigned to free form designs.

In PULL WORK the threads of a loosely woven fabric are *PULL*ed together to create dense and open areas. No threads are removed or cut out.

In DRAWN WORK, select thread are with*DRAWN* and then the remaining threads grouped by various stitches into planned patterns. The original name for this technique as executed in Italy in the 16th c. was PUNTO TIRATO. It has been a popular technique in China, Middle East, India, Mexico, South America and the Philippines where some of the finest work can be found. Each of these areas developed drawnwork expression differently although the basic method was essentially the same. Mexican drawnwork can be characterized by spider web designs while other styles tended to imitate the charted designs of Lacis and Buratto or the flowing free form deigns of richelieu work.

There are two basic concepts of needlework design, *hemstitching* and *needleweaving*. Hemstitching has the widest use and is typically a narrow row of stitches worked around a folded hem. It is also commonly used around a larger drawn worked area to keep the threads in place. Needleweaving involves wider bands and with use of color stitching threads, can be very decorative.

Many of the drawn work designs can be seen in the pure needle laces, particularly in the Teneriffe laces, where threads are woven with a needle in a specific design to accommodate the desired patterns.

MATERIALS

References to materials in this publication are as originally notated in the original turn-of-the-century edition and are not necessarily available today.

A plain even weave fabric (even thread count in both directions) of a loose weave such as a batiste is suggested as the working material although theoretically any woven fabric can be used. The looser the weave the easier to work.

For hemstitching, the infilling or stitching threads should be of a smooth cotton of equivalent weight to that of the woven threads.

For decorative needleweaving, heavier threads such as pearl cotton and embroidery floss can be used in natural as well as threads in contrasting colors.

The principal consideration in doing drawnwork is the correct counting of the threads when drawing them out and when combining them into patterns. For the beginner a hardanger cloth and pearl cotton is suggested.

A blunt pointed tapestry needle, of size suited to the material being used, is preferred for counting and dividing the threads without splitting them, as well as for making the stitches.

Originally published in March, 1896 as Vol 2, No. 1 as part of the "Metropolitan Art Series," a quarterly publication devoted to Crafts and the Needle Arts, by the Butterick Publishing Co., THE ART OF DRAWN WORK is still the most complete work on this area of needlework. Although limited primarily to Mexican Drawn work, the techniques and stitches will be common to all styles of drawn work.

With the exception of the elimination of a page of advertising and the inclusion of additional illustrations, this edition is an unabridged version of the original.

BIBLIOGRAPHY

DURCHBRUCH, Verlag fur die Frau. German text but beautifully illustrated. Includes teneriffe techniques.
DOPPELDURCHBRUCH, Verlag fur die Frau. A second volume with additional techniques.
HOHLSAUME, Eva Maria Leszner. Contemporary ideas.
.... *Publisher*

LACIS
PUBLICATIONS

3163 Adeline Street, Berkeley, CA 94703
© 1989, Jules Kliot

ISBN 0-916896-29-3

2

"The art of a thing is, first, its aim, and next, its manner of accomplishment."—*Bovee.*

"Our knowledge is the amassed thought and experience of innumerable minds."—*Emmerson.*

"* * * * she is not yet so old, but she may learn."—*Shakspeare.*

Drawn-thread Tea-cosy.   Chinese work done in Mission School.

INTRODUCTION.

———◆———

A BOOK of instruction, whether it be for the use of children or adults, amateurs or experts, should be complete. By this we mean that, as far as possible, it should begin at the alphabet, or the rudiments of the subject-matter, and progress step by step to the climax of mastery.

But in preparing books of so-called instruction upon the various branches of art and needle-craft, this necessary point of comprehensiveness is too often either lost sight of entirely or voluntarily neglected on the general taking-it-for-granted principle that everyone knows all about the primary steps of all such occupations or pastimes. The author or compiler, therefore frequently selects a fine array of charming designs for the pages of her book, and leaves its purchasers to find out from some other source, which may or may not be within their reach how to develop and make a practical use of the designs mentioned. This, naturally, is not satisfactory to the possessor of the book, who, if she be a beginner and knows nothing of the first necessary steps of the work she wishes to do, is quite as helpless as she was before she made the purchase.

The pronounced and very gratifying success which has attended the careful and comprehensive preparation of our previously issued pampnlets upon Modern Lace-Making and Crocheting, has proved to us the wisdom of sparing no effort to make each of the series as complete as possible—beginning with the alpha and ending witn an omega, beyond which the clever student will find open fields upon which to build the structures of her own imagination or easily duplicate the material creations of the genius of other originators.

In planning and preparing this pamphlet upon Drawn-Work, the point just mentioned has been kept constantly in view. Beginning with a list of suitable fabrics, knotting materials and implements, and telling how to draw the threads and make the foundation stitch of all drawn-work, we have placed before the student every step of the work from the rudiments to the development of the most elaborate designs ; and of the latter we have selected many noted for their beauty, some of which are intricate in construction and effect, others easy to develop but complicated in appearance, while many are extremely attractive to the eye from their very simplicity of design and construction. The instructions and suggestions found in the book make the development of all of the designs easy of accomplishment, and render the evolution of individual designs an occupation of fascinating interest.

it is not necessary to expatiate upon the thoroughness of the work in this book. Those who glance at its opening pages will at once comprehend that the subject has been treated in an exhaustive manner ; and all of the pages plainly indicate that neither time nor expense has been spared in preparing a work which is the best of its kind ever issued. Nor do we need to instill by words into the minds of mothers and daughters the fact that the contents of this little book will materially assist them in beautifying their homes, for its comparatively few pages silently offer to both the eye and the mind a greater variety of designs in this branch of needle-craft, than tongue or pen could alone describe in days of time or unlimited space. Knowing all this and feeling that our efforts will receive the keenest appreciation, it is with the sincerest pleasure that we offer to our patrons this complete and valuable book upon THE ART OF DRAWN-WORK.

THE BUTTERICK PUBLISHING CO. [Limited].

1896

CONTENTS.

The Art of Drawn-Work.

CHAPTER I.

THE general and popular title for this particular variety of needle-craft is "Spanish" or "Mexican Drawn-Work"; but, while the native needle-women of Spain and Mexico have developed the art to a very high standard of beauty, in neither of these countries did it have its origin. Like lace and embroidery, its first traces were discovered hundreds of years ago when, according to present history, the countries known to man were yet in a primitive condition, and the times were those now referred to as the "dark ages." Even in those days needle-work of various descriptions though of rude construction, was found in the tombs of those who had lived in other centuries even then long since passed.

In the twelfth century the tomb of St. Cuthbert at the Cathedral of Durham was opened, and the monk Reginald, who took part in the ceremonials, writes that the saint's shroud had a fringe of linen threads an inch long, and that this was surmounted by a border "worked upon the threads" with representations of birds and beasts and branching trees. A translation from Lucan's Pharsalia describes a garment of "Sidonian fabric, which, pressed down with the comb (or sley) of the Seres, the needle of the Nile workmen has separated and has loosened the warp by stretching out (or withdrawing) the weft."

An alb (an ecclesiastical vestment worn by the Roman Catholic clergy when saying mass) of linen drawn-thread work, said to have been done by Anne of Bohemia (1527) is still preserved in the Cathedral at Prague; and a specimen of "drawn-thread work" dating back to 1588 shows a leaf design intersected by diagonal bands in which the word *Liberta* is wrought out by means of drawn threads and broidery.

Charles V. owned a cap made of cut-work and embroidery which is really nothing more nor less than a species of drawn-work, now known under various titles, one of which is Danish drawn-work.

Drawn-work was a favorite occupation with Turkish women, and is still very much affected in the harems at Constantinople. It is also in this storied city of the East that thousands of women made refugees by the Russo-Turkish war are now making the beautiful Bulgarian embroideries at present so popular; and a very noticeable feature of many of the finest specimens of Bulgarian work is, that its embroideries are inseparably connected with a drawn-work foundation.

The Italians were noted for their laces and drawn-work, and the latter was often called *punto a gruppo, point tiré, punto reale, punto tirato* and *fili tirati*. On page 56 at No. 13 will be seen the engraving of a specimen of the latter lace or drawn-work which is really *fili tirati*, but is called *punto tirato*. The whole foundation is formed of the undrawn threads of the fabric which are wound with working cotton or linen, while the drawn spaces are filled in by figures composed of lace stitches.

On page 59 at No. 8 is illustrated a fragment of lace or drawn-work of great interest, which was shown and described by the Countess Gigliucci of Romagna. It was found at a villa belonging to her husband near Fermo on the Adriatic, and was supposed to have been begun by his great grandmother nearly two hundred years ago.

Historical records of needle-craft contain, however, very limited information concerning the first drawn-work made. We submit the result of our research more as matters likely to be of interest to our readers than as points establishing the origin of this beautiful work. The date of its introduction must ever hover in the labyrinths of antiquity in spite of the present names by which the multitude of needle-women now designate this fascinating branch of their craft. Its nomenclature, however, in no way affects its methods. They are always the same.

The various merits of the work, which include and combine the useful and the ornamental, have rendered it widely popular; and from the first simple designs of remote periods have been evolved, by the cunning and genius of artistic and skilled brains and hands, most intricate and elaborate present examples of modern drawn-work.

The purposes to which drawn-work is adapted are many, and the woman with a creative mind will constantly discover new uses to add to the list. All descriptions of table, buffet, bureau and bed-linen display it; tidies, handkerchiefs and underwear are beautified by it; and curtains, aprons, robes and couch covers also come within the scope given this ancient though modernly applied decoration.

MATERIALS USED IN DRAWN-WORK.

FABRICS.

The uses just mentioned naturally suggest the fabrics employed. Linen, of course, is the best for most purposes, since its threads are stronger and are, therefore, drawn with less trouble; though even linen must be selected with care, for if its threads are uneven or lumpy they will give endless trouble in drawing, and produce a rough effect when the work is done. A little experience in this respect will soon teach the beginner to detect the difference between the linen she does want and that which she does not.

Linen with a round, smooth thread and as free from dressing as can be obtained will produce the most satisfactory work. Should it be impossible, however, to procure a very soft piece of linen, an ordinary piece may be stretched and pressed between two wet cloths, and then allowed to dry while under tension. Another plan is to pour boiling water over the linen and then spread it in the sun to dry; but this process is not particularly advisable, since it destroys the smooth, satiny finish of the fabric on which the beauty of the work so much depends. In all varieties of linen, from crash, which is best fitted for side-board, dressing-table, bureau and table scarfs, down to linen lawn or grass-linen, which is used for finger-bowl doilies, fine tray-cloths, dainty pillow and bolster slips and toilet-cushion covers, the inequalities of warp and filling will be noticed.

For curtains, aprons, chair-scarfs, tidies, etc., scrim, cheese-cloth, unbleached muslin, cambric, silk, pongee, bolting cloth, canvas or any material of a soft, loose weave may be used, the discretion and taste of the worker largely directing the selection of the fabric.

THE COTTON OR THREAD.

This may be white or colored, as the taste and work may decide, but white is most generally used. Linen thread, white and colored, is used a great deal upon linen, as is also colored cotton; but crochet cotton in numbers from 8 to 20 generally produces the most satisfactory work. Occasionally, for some fancy article, silk is used upon linen, with very good effect. It is known as "wash embroidery silk" and comes in all the brilliant and delicate hues of the other silks. In hemstitching, the threads should be so fine that when the work is completed the stitches will be almost invisible. This is particularly desirable when the article is a handkerchief or a toilet-cushion cover, both of which are usually made of linen lawn of the sheerest quality, and often of mull.

DRAWING THE THREADS.

The material chosen, the next important step

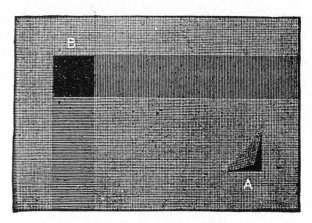

No. 1.—Process of Drawing Threads.

will be the drawing of the threads. Counting them to make the drawn spaces equal seems to be a theory popularly accepted as correct, but except when the material is of the nature of scrim—perfectly even in its weave—measuring is by far the better plan. Sometimes the threads of the warp are a trifle heavier than those of the filling, and it can at once be seen that were a square opening desired, drawing an equal number of threads from opposite directions would not produce it. A perfect square of paper laid on the material would prove, by counting the threads of the fabric, that several more would be required from one direction than the other to make the square perfect. This will also be found true of spaces which are to be alike; hence in all fine fabrics, measuring will result in more accuracy of effect than counting.

No. 1.—Process of Drawing Threads.—This engraving shows how to cut a corner (A) from which to draw the threads each way to produce the effect at (B) and leave a continuous border of the material. The principle thus explained may be applied to the cutting of any design preparatory to mounting the work upon the frame. The ordinary method of drawing the threads is from side to side, leaving a block of the material at each corner, as may be seen by a reference to the work stretched in the frame at No. 3 on page 9.

FRAMES FOR DRAWN-WORK.

Having cut and drawn the threads, how to do the work properly becomes the question, for unless smoothly done it is sure to be a failure from an artistic point, and even people with an uncultivated eye for its beauties must acknowledge its lack of finish and other faults. It must, except in hemstitching, be stretched upon a square or oblong frame, or drawn smoothly over a thin hoop and there tightly held by another passed over the first one and the material, as shown by No. 2 on this page. These hoops may be purchased at any fancy store; and should they not fit tightly when the work is adjusted, which they must, one or both should be wound with ribbon or tape or a strip of thin muslin.

No. 3 shows the usual square embroidery-

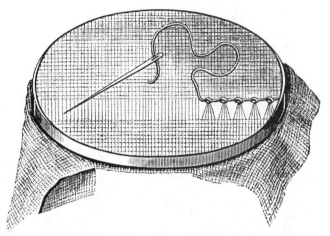

No. 2.—HOOP-FRAME, WITH WORK ADJUSTED.

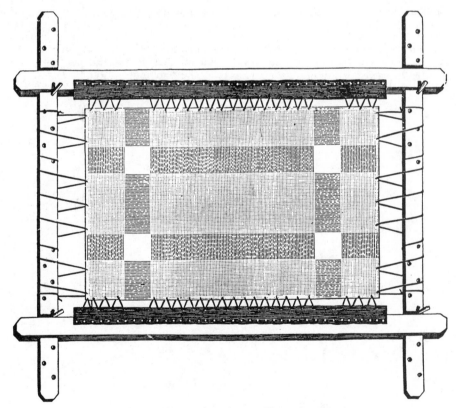

No. 3.—SQUARE FRAME, WITH WORK ADJUSTED.

frame with the work properly fastened on. A strip of webbing or heavy muslin is tacked to each of the thick sides of the frame, and to these strips the sides of the work are first sewed as represented. The end sticks are then inserted, and as they are provided with small holes into which wooden pegs must be fitted, the work may be stretched as tightly as desired and held so until finished. After these end-sticks are inserted and secured, the ends or remaining sides of the work are sewed to them as illustrated. If it is not possible to procure one of the regular embroidery-frames, a slate or any other flat frame may be utilized by smoothly winding it with muslin, as represented at No. 4 on this page, where the method of winding and a section of a wound frame are given. The sides of the work are sewn to the wound sides of such a frame, which in many instances exceeds in convenience the usefulness of the frames sold expressly for needle-work. For very dainty work a frame of the size and shape required may be cut from stiff pasteboard and wound with muslin, and will be found to answer every requirement. Many ladies prefer to do their hemstitching with a frame instead of without, as the result in all drawn work is generally better when the fabric is stretched tightly. A hem can be held very smoothly over the fingers, however.

Round and square frames of various sizes may

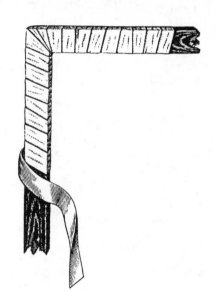

NO. 4.—SECTION OF HOME-MADE FRAME.

be purchased, the hoops from three to eighteen inches in diameter, and the others from a very small size to one sufficiently large for most pieces of work. But for large articles, such as tea-cloths, lunch-cloths, robes and spreads, it will be necessary to have one made by a carpenter; or to quarter the work and stretch one quarter of it at a time, rolling and securing the rest neatly to keep it from becoming soiled before the piece is finished. Stretch all work very tightly and very evenly in the frames, which must be heavy enough to resist the strain. This is often difficult to do, but any time spent upon its accomplishment will be more than compensated for by the appearance of the work when completed. Frames have wholly superseded cushions, upon which, at one time the work used to be stretched and pinned.

Having thoroughly discussed uses, materials, implements and general necessary preliminaries, we will next give the initial foundation stitches, and in the pages immediately following the remaining stitches, describing the method and application of each as it appears.

CHAPTER II.

STITCHES USED IN DRAWN-WORK.

KNOT STITCH.

No. 1.—The foundation stitch of all drawn-work, and also of Spanish lace-work is here represented.

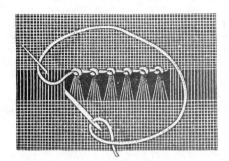

NO. 1.—KNOT STITCH.

It is called the "knot stitch," and a succession of such stitches is called a "knot chain." The latter is the first method of producing a hemstitch effect where no hem occurs. In making this stitch the thread is carried to the left, then upward to the right, thus forming a loop, as will be seen by referring to the engraving. The needle is then inserted

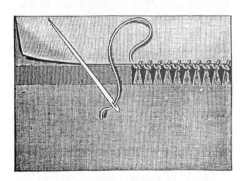

NO. 2.—THE KNOT HEMSTITCH.

under the drawn threads to be tied, and the working thread is passed upward through the loop. The thread is then carefully drawn to produce the

knot seen in the engraving. This part of the work may require some practice, since it is essential that the knot be neatly made, and to do it neatly will require the thorough understanding resulting from many repetitions of the movement. The number of drawn threads to be taken up by a knot must be decided by taste and effect. Different grades of material and spaces of varying widths will necessitate the taking up of a greater or less number of threads. Having personally decided upon the number, the beginner in drawn-work will find it to her advantage to count the threads for some time; but she will be surprised to see how soon she will be able to equally gauge the strands she wishes to knot without counting. The knot stitch is a very firm one and is better adapted to articles of the "wear and tear" class than any of the others em-

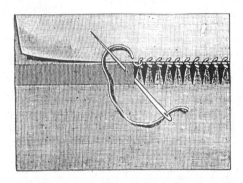

NO. 3.—HEMSTITCH. (SECOND METHOD.)

ployed in knotting the drawn threads or hemstitching, though it is a little more difficult to make. Fancy drawn-work is very pretty done in colored threads, and sometimes two colors will be used, such as red and blue, or yellow and blue.

Having mastered the knot stitch the ambitious needle-woman may now consider herself competent to apply it in various ways to the work she has in view. If she wishes to hem a garment, a handkerchief, a tidy or a scarf, using this stitch, she may do so without difficulty, by following the instructions given for No. 2.

THE KNOT HEMSTITCH.

No. 2.—The first step in hemstitching is to

draw the threads, twice the width of the hem wanted, from the edge. Then prepare the hem in the ordinary way, but baste it smoothly down, with its turned-under edge even with the upper edge of

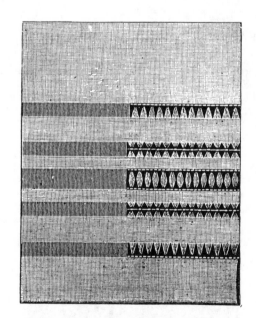

No. 4.—Section of Hemstitch Design.

the drawn space. A frame is not really needed for hemstitching, and the work is held as most convenient for the worker. Some people hold the folded hem next to, and others away from, them. The latter method is represented, but so long as the correct stitch is obtained the position of the work is immaterial.

The threads are taken up by the knot stitch described at No. 1 on page 11, and after each stitch is made the needle is passed up under the edge of the hem, as seen in the present illustration ; then the next knot stitch is made, and these details are repeated until the end of the hem is reached. A second method is given below, but the one just described is the more durable and is much used for hemstitching underwear and household linen.

HEMSTITCH. (Second Method.)

No. 3.—This is the easier method of the two and may be much more quickly done ; therefore, it is most commonly employed when the question of durability does not enter into consideration. In this method the thread is first drawn to the left, then downward to the right, as seen in the illustration, and the needle is inserted underneath the drawn threads and passed up through the loop thus formed. The second step of this hemstitch is identical with that in the first, the needle being

passed up under the fold of the hem before the next knot is made.

SECTION OF HEMSTITCH DESIGN.

No. 4.—This engraving represents the two varieties of hemstitching—the upper two drawn rows showing the knot-chain method and the lower two the second method, with the intermediate stitch taken up through the material the same as if it were the folded edge of a hem. As the stitches must be made along an *upper edge* of the drawn lines, for every alternate row of them, the work will have to be turned so that the *left* edge is at the *right-hand* side. This will make, for the time being, an *upper* edge of each *lower* edge of the drawn lines. The ends of the working threads are pictured in the engraving to show where each row is finished, so that a mistake in that direction cannot occur if the instructions are followed.

COMPLETE HEMSTITCH DESIGN.

No. 5.—A full or complete design in hemstitch for decorating any of the articles before mentioned, upon which such a decoration can be applied is here given. With the exception of the

No. 5.—Complete Hemstitch Design.

second and fourth lines, the details have been made perfectly clear, and no difficulty will be experienced in reproducing the design. In the spaces excepted it will be seen that the stitches are knotted through the center instead of at the top ; this produces what is called a "duck's trail," and the "knot chain" is employed in making it. This

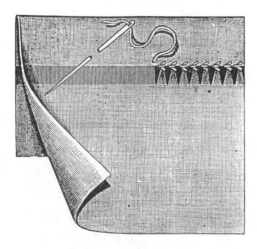

No. 6.—Method of Hemstitching a Tuck.

entire design is very pretty for children's skirts and dresses when fine material is used for them.

METHOD OF HEMSTITCHING A TUCK.

No. 6.—Tucks, always a neat finish for many garments, especially those for children, may be made very ornamental by the hemstitch process. When you have decided upon the width of tuck you wish, draw two rows of thread, *twice the width of the tuck apart*—that is, the *inner edges* of the drawn rows must be *twice the width* apart. Make each drawn row from an eighth to a quarter of an inch wide, according to the fineness of the fabric. When the weave is even the threads drawn may be counted, the same number being drawn from each row ; but in fine textures the plan of measuring heretofore suggested is the better one. When the threads are drawn, double the fabric so that the drawn rows will come exactly together, as seen in the engraving, and baste it firmly. Then on the

under side of the tuck, do the hemstitching through both drawn rows at once, by the stitch described and illustrated at No. 3 ; when the hemstitching is done, turn the tuck down and with the thumb-nail smooth it into place.

COMPLETED HEMSTITCHED TUCK.

No. 7.—This engraving shows the tuck completed and turned down, and also how effective it is when hemstitched neatly. In the next set or design a section of tucking above an ornamental border, which is very pretty when used for an apron or a child's dress will be presented. Tucks alone, when hemstitched, may be arranged in groups of three or five, and in this event a wide hem, also hemstitched, is a suitable finish in the way of a border. White thread or cotton of proper fineness for the fabric is the most refined selection, though often colored working cottons—red, blue or yellow—are chosen by way of

No. 7.—Completed Hemstitched Tuck.

variety, when a number of garments or articles are to be made. These colors are liked on children's dresses of washable goods.

CHAPTER III.

FANCY DESIGNS IN DRAWN-WORK.

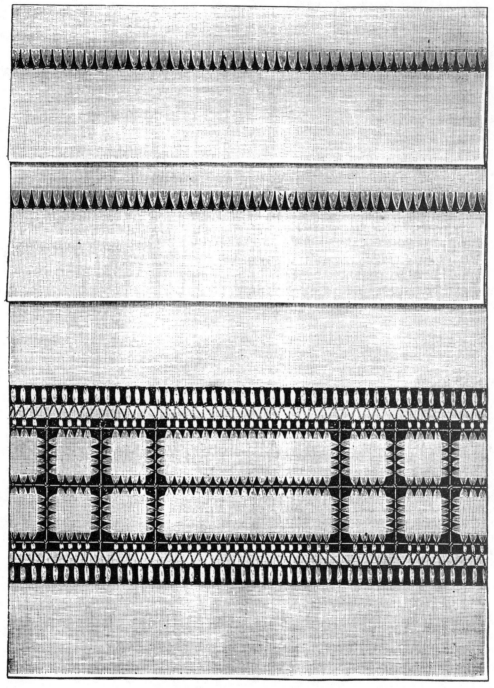

No. 1.—FANCY DESIGN IN DRAWN-WORK.

In this chapter three designs are presented, two of them including portions of the designs seen in the preceding chapter, together with a heading which is very generally used in drawn-work decorations; while the third introduces fancy knotting and its details.

The design seen at No. 1 on the preceding page is very pretty for skirts, aprons and dresses,

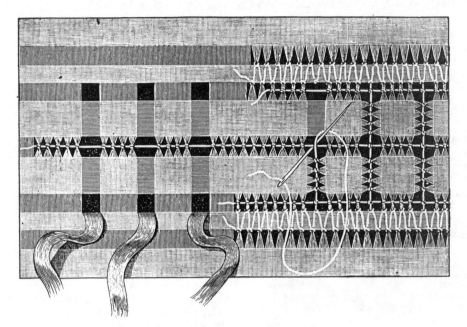

NO. 2.—FANCY DESIGN IN DRAWN-WORK, WITH DETAILS.

or for the robes of infants and the little slips worn by children.

FANCY DESIGN IN DRAWN-WORK.

No. 1.—The design here given shows how handsomely a skirt may be ornamented with drawn-work. The details given at No. 2 were followed in developing the border, while those for the tucking and hem given in a previous chapter were adopted for completing the work. In order to make the upper edge of the top-finish correspond with the edge along the hem, the knot chain by which both are done is made on the under side of the work. The drawn-work may be used as an insertion between clusters of tucks, or feather or other fancy stitching may be made along either edge of it, or between the tucks above it, with charming effect.

FANCY DESIGN IN DRAWN-WORK, WITH DETAILS.

No. 2.—The engraving illustrates a section of a fancy design, and also the manner in which the threads must be drawn to prepare for the knotting. The spaces are all made by drawing an equal number of threads each way of the fabric, and at regular distances apart. The lengthwise threads drawn are closely cut with fine, sharp scissors across the inner edges of the heading, the loose strands in the engraving showing how they are

drawn and where they are to be clipped. When the spaces are drawn, work the finish at each side of the pattern as described at figure No. 3, taking up the *edge*, where the strands are clipped away, in

order to prevent it from ravelling and also to preserve the regularity of the work. Then go over the other drawn spaces, through their centers, with the knot-chain, to form the "duck's-trail" effect described in the preceding chapter. At the square open spaces knot the thread at the center of each, in the manner indicated by the needle and cotton shown in the engraving.

This design may be varied in any manner to

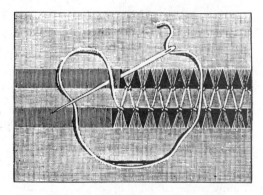

NO. 3.—FINISH, OR HEADING FOR FANCY DESIGN IN DRAWN-WORK.

suit the taste by drawing the threads to form different spaces, blocks or rows; and it may be used upon any article of wear or use that comes within the scope of such ornamentation

FINISH, OR HEADING FOR FANCY DESIGN IN DRAWN-WORK.

No. 3.—As a finish or heading seems to be a part of most decorations, a pretty one for drawn-work is

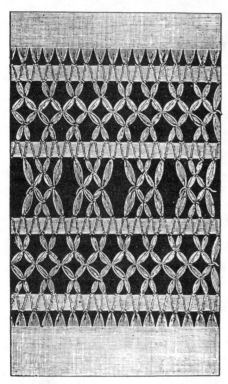

No. 4.—Design for a Border in Drawn-Work.

an important factor, and the one illustrated at No. 3 on the preceding page is a very popular design.

The threads are drawn as pictured in the engraving, the intermediate space occupied by the undrawn threads being a thread or two wider than the drawn spaces. The latter are both alike and may be measured, or, if the material permits, the threads to be drawn may be counted. The knot stitch is used in tying the strands, and the cotton is carried back and forth from one side of the middle space to the other, so that the latter is overlaid by it when the work is completed. The engraving shows how the strands are taken up and the cotton is carried to form the knot, which has been fully described in the preceding chapter. It will be observed that each knotting of the upper edge comes between the two knottings of the lower edge beneath it. In order to do this accurately, an even number of threads must be counted for each strand; then, when the lower strands are knotted, each should be composed of *half* the number of threads in each of the *two* strands *over* it. After knotting two or three strands in this way, the method will become perfectly plain and easy, and the work will progress rapidly.

This finish will be found very effective when

produced at each edge of any chosen design; or it may form a dainty addition by itself, being made at some distance from a border of different work. In colored cotton it is very pretty for tidies, towels, scarfs, lunch cloths or any article of household linen; but for garments, handkerchiefs, etc., etc., white cotton or linen is generally used.

DESIGN FOR A BORDER IN DRAWN-WORK.

No. 4.—This engraving represents another very handsome design for a border for under-garments, aprons, towels, tidies, etc. It is totally different in effect from the design shown at No. 1, although some of the details are identical in both. Ribbon is sometimes run through the openings, for fancy articles, but as a rule, the work is daintier in effect when left as shown in the engraving. A dash of color may be supplied by using colored cotton for the knotting instead of white, though the latter is always a refined choice. In preparing the fabric for the knotting, three spaces, each about five-eighths of an inch wide, are made by drawing the threads, and these spaces are separated by two undrawn spaces each a little more than an-eighth of an inch wide. A narrow drawn space is made at the top and bottom of the border, and two more narrow undrawn spaces are thus formed, making four undrawn spaces in all, each of which is overwrought by the stitch and method described at No. 3. This leaves the three broad spaces, the strands of which are then carefully drawn into the effective groupings pictured in the engraving, by following the methods delineated by the remaining illustrations and clearly explained in their corresponding descriptions.

DETAILS FOR BORDER.

Nos. 5, 6, 7, 8 and 9—After the strands have

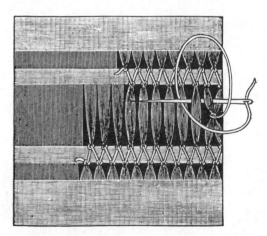

No. 5.—Detail for Border

been knotted according to the instructions for No. 3, the first two strands are knotted together at the middle, and the cotton is carried upward and then over to the left and back to the right, to form a loop. The needle is then slipped under the cotton and the *second* and *third* strands and through the loop, as seen at No. 5, and is drawn through, knotting the cotton as seen at No. 6. The latter engraving shows the next step of the work, which is to bring the cotton down, then to the left and up over to the right, to form a loop; the needle is then inserted under it and the *second* and *third* strands and through the loop as illustrated, and is

This design appears at the upper and lower edges of the border illustrated by No. 4, and it will be observed that each grouping appears to be formed by two strands, though four are really used to complete the first grouping. This effect is the result of connecting the groupings instead of making each separately like those seen through the center of the border. The details for the latter are sufficiently illustrated at No. 9 to enable the worker, who by this time has mastered the movements of the other groupings, to make them without diffi

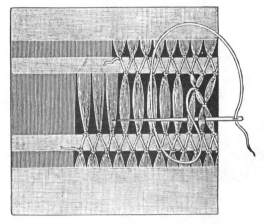

No. 6

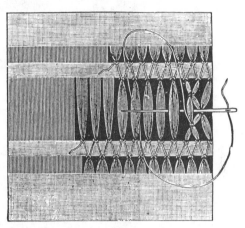

No. 7.

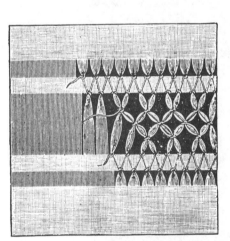

No. 8.

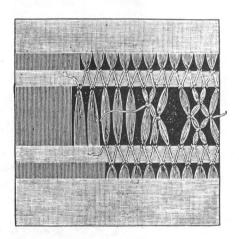

No. 9.

NOS. 6, 7, 8 AND 9.—DETAILS FOR BORDER.

drawn through, knotting the cotton as shown by No. 7. This engraving also shows the final step of this design. After making the last knot, the cotton is carried upward and to the left, and then downward to the right to form the loop. The needle is then slipped under it and the *third* and *fourth* strands, and drawn through the loop to tie the fourth and last knot of the first group.

No. 8 shows a series of completed groups and the method by which a succeeding group is begun.

2

culty, since all the loops and knots are made like those just described, and each group is completed by the fourth knot. The cotton is then brought down to the "finish," at the back of the work, and invisibly caught and carried along to the next two strands, which it unites. The knotting is then proceeded with as before. When the material is tightly stretched on a frame, the work may be quickly and readily done, and it proves as easy as at first it appeared intricate and difficult.

CHAPTER IV.

EDGE DESIGN IN DRAWN-WORK.

No. 1.—Edge Design in Drawn-Work.

By this time the student of drawn-work has discovered that its delicate and lace-like designs are very easy to develop; for as a child, learning to read, finds the task comparatively simple after the alphapet has been mastered, so the novice in this branch of needle-work meets with little difficulty after she has learned its alphabet, which consists of two or three kinds of knot stitches. The possibilities of the work are numerous, and as it progresses each learner will find that her individual taste will suggest combinations that will be quite as pretty as the various patterns given here. The scope of their application will also broaden, and a great many articles not specified on these pages

tidies, etc., and, despite its elaborate effect, it is really quite easy to reproduce. A design based upon a foundation of similar detail was given in chapter III. at No. 4, and those of our students who mastered that design will find this one very simple.

DETAILS FOR THE TUCKS.

No. 2.—In making the tucks shown at No. 1, the

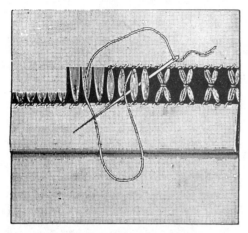

No. 2.—DETAILS FOR THE TUCKS.

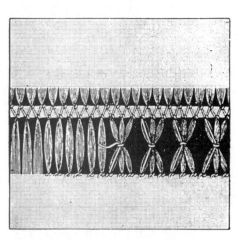

No. 3.

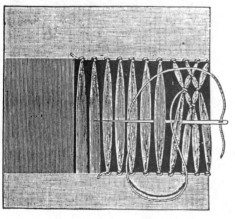

No. 4.

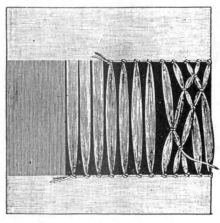

No. 5.

NOS. 3, 4 AND 5.—DETAILS FOR EDGE DESIGN.

will present themselves to the worker's mind as adapted to this kind of ornamentation.

EDGE DESIGN IN DRAWN-WORK.

No. 1.—This engraving represents a design for the lower edges of dresses, skirts, aprons, scarfs,

following details must be observed: The threads are drawn and the hemstitching done as directed at Nos. 6 and 7, page 13; then about twice as many more threads are drawn at the top of the strands, as will be observed by examining the engraving. The upper edge of the drawn space is now finished with a row of hemstitching, which draws the strands into position at the top of the space; and the strands are then knotted together in pairs as illustrated. The cotton is carried from under the tuck to the middle of the space, where the first two strands are knotted together by the movement described at No. 5 on page 16, and also illustrated by the arrangement of the needle and cotton here pictured. The cotton is then carried up the side of the strand, and caught as lightly as possible to the under side of the fabric at the top of the space. It is next carried along, still at the back of the work, to the left edge of the fourth strand, and from thence is carried downward to the middle of the space, then brought to the right side of the work and thrown into the position seen in the engraving, to form a loop through which to pass the needle. The loop, being drawn taut, forms the knot that ties every pair of the strands together; and when coming upward from the tuck, the cotton

No. 3, page 19 (which represents the knotting of the upper and lower lines of the border in No. 1), have been separated on the wrong side of the work by the hemstitch known as the "Second Method" and illustrated at No. 3 in chapter II. The knotting of the strands is done precisely like that described at No. 2, page 19, except that three strands instead of two are tied by each knot. Nos. 4, 5, 6 and 7 are intended simply to show the details of the knotting of the middle section of the border, and are so perfectly arranged that specific directions are unnecessary, since by this time the worker is thoroughly accustomed to knotting strands and can do it simply by the eye from any pattern given. It will be observed that the strands of the border are separated by two undrawn spaces overlaid by the heading stitch, which connects the strands at both sides of each; and that the knotting

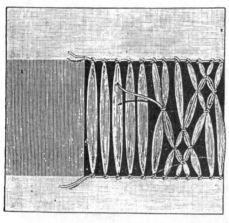

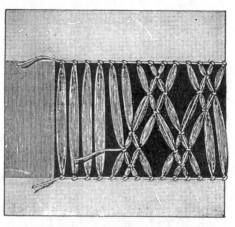

No. 6.   No. 7.

NOS. 6 AND 7.—DETAILS FOR EDGE DESIGN.

must be brought up and over, to form a similar loop. The knotting throughout the large design is performed in this same manner, and its hem is made with the stitch illustrated and described at No. 3, in chapter II.

DETAILS FOR EDGE DESIGN.

NOS. 3, 4, 5, 6 AND 7.—These engravings delineate the remainder of the details for the design, and are sufficiently plain in themselves to perfectly instruct the worker. No. 3 includes a heading, which is omitted from the top of the border in the large design, but may be added to either edge of it. This heading has been fully described at No. 3, page 15. The strands at the top of the space in

is so arranged that the strands of the middle row come between those of the other two rows. But the strands of the "details" are separated by the knot chain. The knot chain may be used where the middle row of the border is to form the decoration without additional ornamentation. In the latter event the knot hemstitch will prove an admirable fastening for the strands, since it will not slip away from the edge, as the knot chain possibly may.

Except in a few instance, it is advisable to do all drawn-work with white cotton, as the effect is more refined; and if the article ornamented is to be subjected to frequent laundering, it will always come forth from the operation clean and clear, without any faded tints and with none of the strands disfigured by running colors.

CHAPTER V.

DESIGN FOR A BORDER IN DRAWN-WORK.

No. 1.—DESIGN FOR A BORDER IN DRAWN-WORK.

The design and its details represented by the following engravings, which are fully explained, will prove a charming decoration for any article or garment admitting of a border finish, and especially those made of coarse linen and other washable fabrics. While time and patience will be required to produce it perfectly, the worker will find most of the details of the pattern already within her possession, if she has mastered the instructions for the drawn-work given on the previous pages.

DESIGN FOR A BORDER IN DRAWN-WORK.

No. 1.—This engraving represents the design mentioned. It will be observed that the middle

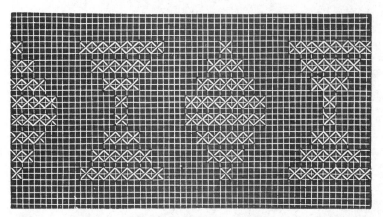

No. 2.—Cross-Stitch Design.

pattern is worked out by the details of Nos. 8 and 9, in chapter III. In knotting that part of it represented by No. 8, twenty strands will be required for every section so knotted; for the knotting done by No. 9, twenty-eight strands will be required for each *outside row* of clusters forming the cone-shaped sections, and twenty-eight for the *two middle* rows of each diamond-shaped section. Each apex of the latter section contains only four strands or one cluster. An ordinary cross-stitch pattern, such as is used for canvas work, formed the basis of this design, and we give it for the benefit of our readers, with the information that its crosses represent one set of clusters, and the spaces are to be taken up by the other set, as shown in the engraving of the completed design. Other patterns in cross-stitch may be worked out in the same manner; or, other styles of knottings may be selected, Nos. 2 and 7 in chapter IV., for instance, forming a charming combination with which to incorporate a cross-stitch pattern.

CROSS–STITCH DESIGN.

No. 2.—This engraving shows the pattern by which the middle portion of No. 1 was knotted, and its purpose has necessarily been fully explained in the description of No. 1.

It will, of course, be understood that spaces are to be drawn of the width that appears most suitable to the fabric being decorated, and that this part of the process must be regulated by personal judgment. An inspection of No. 1 will clearly disclose how many spaces must be drawn, and their relative distances from each other. When the

spaces are drawn the fabric must be tightly stretched upon the frame, and the threads then separated into strands, This practically makes a canvas of the work and renders it very easy to apply to it the cross-stitch pattern. In the samples from which these illustrations were made butcher's linen was the fabric employed, and the drawn spaces of the central part of the design were about half an inch wide, and those of the central part of its border were each about three-eighths of an inch in width. The undrawn, narrower spaces were an-eighth of an inch wide, and the wider ones just a trifle more. By referring to No. 1 the worker will be easily able to apply the border, since its details, given at Nos. 3, 4 and 5, are clearly represented and described; and it will also be observed that in No. 5 a new and pleasing method of separating the strands is given, and may be employed instead of the one heretofore illustrated. It is not quite as strong as the method first given for washable articles, but is very pretty. It is

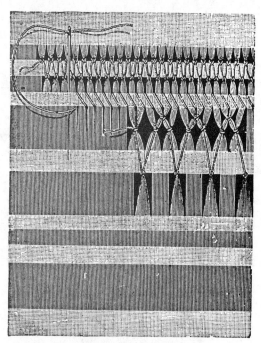

No. 3.—Detail of Outer Border.

only incidentally mentioned here, but will be properly described in its regular order.

DETAILS OF OUTER BORDER.

Nos. 3, 4 AND 5.—These three engravings represent the details of the border seen at the top and bottom of the design at No. 1. The method of drawing the threads is made clear by all three, and the upper row of knotting is familiar by this time to all our students and needs no further explana-

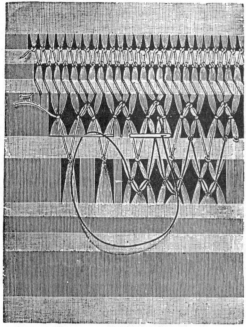

No. 4.

tion. The second process almost imperceptibly divides the strands for further knotting, but at the same time it prettily covers the narrow, un-drawn space. It is plainly explained in the engraving, which shows the manner of setting the needle, and the fall of the thread, as well as the result, and words could not make it more apparent. Then comes the next knotting, which, so far as each knot itself is concerned, is done exactly like all the knotting of the previous work illustrated; but the uniting of the strands is quite different from anything given heretofore, and is unique as well as pretty. Looking at the illustration it will be seen that the *first* knot made, ties what would make two strands in the *lower* of the two wide spaces. The thread is then carried up to the middle of the upper space, where it knots together *two* strands, one of which forms the *second* strand of the first knotting in the lower space; it is then carried a little higher and knots together the *second* of the two first strands in the same space, and a *third* strand, and then comes back to the center, knotting this *third* strand to a *fourth*, after which it is carried down to the top of the *lower* space; and after the threads of the *second* and *third* strands above are skipped, another strand is taken up which includes the threads of the *fourth* and *fifth* strands of the *upper* space. This forms the knotting of one cluster in the upper space and two double strands of the lower; and the details given are applied to the knotting of all the other clusters in the row to the end of the work.

No. 4 shows the next step of the work after what is illustrated by No. 3 has been completed. It simply reverses the latter process and forms the clusters this time in the lower space, but arranges them so that every cluster in the *lower* space comes between two in the *upper* space. It also shows how to take up the two middle strands in each cluster of the upper space, after every cluster in the lower one is finished. Contrary to the regular rule for throwing the thread for the knot stitch, the thread is here carried *downward* to the right, but since the result is the same, the deviation does not signify. The work appears elaborate, but it will be seen that it is quite simple and may be done very rapidly after a little practice. If desired, these details may be developed alone as a decoration, without being connected with the center of the design.

No. 5 shows the outer border fully completed. The lower row of the work is done by the new method previously mentioned. Each strand is taken up as illustrated, the needle passing under it and over the thread, and this direction applies to both the top and bottom of the row. No knot is made. The thread forms a single *twist* which holds each strand loosely, but at the same time quite firmly, since the thread, in crossing back and forth, prevents it slipping away to any extent from the strands of either side.

For children's dresses, and for skirts, aprons and gowns for older persons as well, this is an exceed-

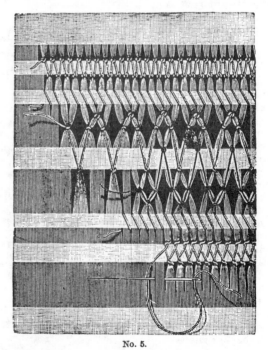

No. 5.

NOS. 4 AND 5.—DETAILS OF OUTER BORDER.

ingly dainty pattern. It may also be used through the center of a buffet or bureau scarf, or upon tidies, towels, sheets, pillow and bolster cases or undergarments of various descriptions.

CHAPTER VI.

DESIGN FOR A TOWEL-BORDER.

Given plenty of time, a taste for the employment and even the few examples of drawn-work thus far illustrated, and what a field of possibilities opens out before the student of this decorative art! All the designs presented have been very pretty, the present one being exceptionally so; but the learner must not feel obliged to confine all her efforts to an exact reproduction of the details she has mastered in her lessons. She may combine a part of one pattern with some pretty portion of another; or, as in the design in the preceding chapter, she may follow some striking canvas-work pattern, selecting any of the fancy knottings heretofore given for carrying out the effect. In fact, so long as she preserves correctness in the foundation stitches, her privilege in the matter of combination is limitless, and she may thus deftly work out her own ideal upon the dainty strands.

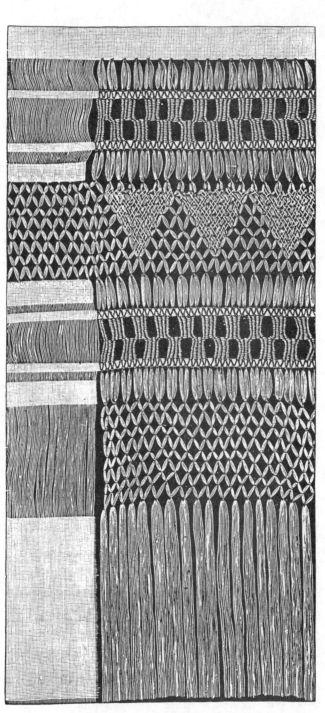

No. 1.—DESIGN FOR A TOWEL-BORDER.

DESIGN FOR A TOWEL-BORDER.

No. 1.—This engraving represents a pattern designed especially for bordering towels, although it may be tastefully employed for bureau-scarfs, tidies, lunch and tea-cloths or for any article that may be appropriately completed with a fringe; or if a hem supplies the edge-finish, the design may be applied to aprons, skirts and dresses. The points in the upper row of net-work are darned in, and any of the patterns used for the solid portions of darned net-work may be substituted for the points. The simple but pretty solid portions of torchon or Smyrna laces may also be copied for darning the netted portions of drawn-work, and it may be done with white or colored cotton, as preferred.

In preparing the material for this border, the method pictured at the left of the engraving must be followed for very apparent reasons. If the threads were all drawn before any of the work was done, it can be easily comprehended that it would be almost impossible to keep the upper and lower knottings of the netted portions even or on

pleted, the darning is made; the top of the upper space is drawn into strands, as represented, by any preferred variety of the several knot or hem stitches; and the threads remaining at each side of the netting above and below the narrow headings and below the lower netting are then drawn, thus completing the design from the upper edge to the fringe. It will be observed that at the *upper edge* of the border *two* strands are knotted together each time to preserve the effect produced by the knotting of the netted portions.

DETAILS FOR THE NET-WORK.

NOS. 2, 3 AND

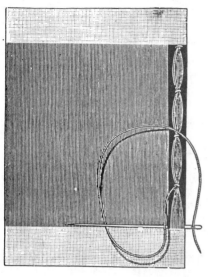

No. 2.

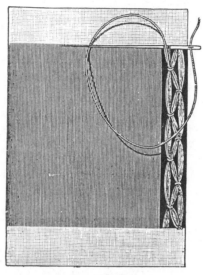

No. 3.

a straight line. Therefore, the whole space is calculated for, but for the upper row of knotting only a few threads are drawn at each side of the calculated space —just enough to permit the strands to be knotted by the stitches crossing the narrow heading below and above the block work. The spaces to be occupied by the *netted portions* are next drawn, and a sufficient depth of undrawn material is left below the lowest drawn space, as seen in the engraving for a fringe of graceful length. All the spaces having been prepared, the fabric is fastened smoothly and accurately to the frame and the work done according to the following details: After the netted portions are com-

No. 4.

NOS. 2, 3 AND 4.—DETAILS FOR THE NET-WORK.

4.—After the space for it has been prepared, as described and illustrated at No. 1, the knotting is begun as shown at No. 2. Catch the working thread at the top of the space, bring it down about one-fourth the depth of the space, and knot together a group of threads sufficient in number to make two ordinary strands, using the knotting process shown by the arrangement of the needle and thread in the engraving. This process is the same as that hitherto illustrated, and is repeated three times more in order to produce four spaces along the group of threads. The working thread is then carried upward to a point opposite the middle of the lowest space, and another group containing *half as many threads as the first group* is here knotted to the *second half* of the *first* group, the picture of the needle and thread in No. 3 fully explaining the process. There are now *three* strands knotted together. A similar knotting is made at the middle of each space and one at the top of the drawn portion. This gives *three* whole spaces, which alternate with the four first made. A fourth strand is now joined to the third by the process used in knotting the first spaces, and another is joined by the process of the second knotting; and these two rows are repeated until the network is completed. The rest of the threads to be drawn are then removed, after which the narrow heading lines are made by knotting across the heading in the usual way the threads at each side of it. In knotting the strands of the net-work, it will be observed that they are separated and taken up so as to come between the strands at the other side of the heading. The points are next darned in by the regular over-and-under darning process. In this case the darning is so clearly represented by the engraving that detailed instructions are not needed—in fact, they would undoubtedly confuse a beginner, who will, however, be able to darn the points perfectly from an inspection of the engraving. In turning at the top of the points it will be well to make a knot just at the turn, to provide against a possible slipping of the working thread when the article is laundered.

DESIGN FOR THE BLOCK-WORK FINISH.

No. 5.—This finish appears as a heading to the net-work, but it may be used as a separate ornamentation for any article or as a heading to any other design. When the space for it has been divided into strands by the knottings which cross the narrow undrawn spaces, as represented

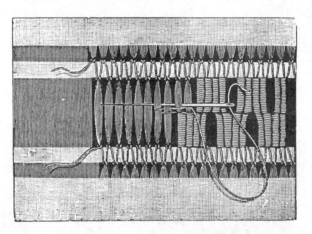

No. 5.—DESIGN FOR THE BLOCK-WORK FINISH.

in the engraving, proceed as follows: Begin close to the upper edge of the space, and by the over and under movement, back and forth, darn together the first two strands for half the width of the space. Then take up the next two strands, and darn the *four* together to the bottom of the space. Run the darning thread in some invisible way up to the middle of the space where the second two strands were taken up, and darn the upper half of the second two strands with the same half of the *next* two strands. Follow this method across the work, taking up two new strands in darning the upper and lower halves of each preceding two strands. A movement or two of the darning thread is represented, and the needle is also set in the strands as they are to be taken up by it, thus fully explaining the whole process.

It will be seen that the fringe is quite as effective as when each strand of it is knotted in the orthodox way, and that this plan of making it is far easier and more simple. The fringe is the last part made, and when it is all ravelled it may be combed out upon some flat surface and then clipped with the scissors to make it perfectly even, if necessary.

In this design it would be a very good plan to adopt the following systematic methods: First draw the threads as directed, and then fasten the fabric to the frame. Next make the network, and draw the remaining threads. Darn in the points, and then knot all the strands by the stitch used in making the narrow heading, also knotting the strands at the top of the border. Next make the block-work finish, and finally ravel out the fringe.

This border is very pretty when made with colored working-thread, which may be used throughout the design or only in portions of it. The block-work is very effective when done in red cotton, the remainder of the work being white; or the points may also be darned in red or whatever color is selected for the block-work; or the points and narrow headings may be worked in color. A pretty combination results from the use of white linen and unbleached thread. Individual taste will supply many ideas as to color and combination and also suggest applications of various stitches and knottings to the ornamentation of many articles coming within the scope of this decoration.

CHAPTER VII.

BORDER DESIGN IN DRAWN-WORK.

One of the handsomest as well as the most difficult patterns in drawn-work is illustrated and described in the present chapter. It is appropriate for the ornamentation of any of the articles or garments heretofore suggested, and may also be used in producing lace-like effects on fine fabrics, in connection with insertions and edgings or frills of just mentioned and displays its artistic features to good advantage. Considerable skill will be necessary to nicely produce the curves of the knotting threads, but as practice makes perfect, time and patience only will be needed to make the repeated efforts through which the skill required may be obtained. The pattern consists of two

No. 1.—BORDER DESIGN IN DRAWN-WORK.

Valenciennes, torchon, Medici or any fashionable lace used in the decoration of undergarments or fancy articles.

BORDER DESIGN IN DRAWN-WORK.

No. 1.—This engraving represents the pattern distinct designs, and both are made by the same method differently applied. The center is made first. After the space needed for it has been drawn, the material is fastened into a frame and the threads knotted into strands at the top and bottom by the knot chain; this forms the straight line of knotting which is seen in the engraving between the center and the finish at each side, and which is left in this position by drawing the finish-threads *after* the middle design is completed. (A refer-

NO. 2.—DETAIL FOR BORDER DESIGN.

ence to No. 4 will show how these finish-threads are drawn.) If this knot-chain were not used, a narrow heading would have to be made in its place to hold the strands in their proper position. When the center design is finished the work is removed from the frame, the finish threads are drawn, and a hem is made at each side by the "Second Method," illustrated at No. 3 in chapter II., the strands being divided off by the knot chain made at the edges of the center space. After making the hems, the work is secured in the frame once more, and the finish at each side is made. The center design alone may be used in decorating many articles; or the finish may be made at each side of a plain strip or any of the designs previously given. In fact, there is scarcely a limit to the pretty combinations that may be made with the designs that have been and will be given in this book.

DETAILS FOR BORDER DESIGN.

NOS. 2, 3 AND 4.—The first step in making the central part of the design is represented at No. 2. After the knot-chain has been used to tie the strands at the top and bottom, an even number of strands are knotted together at the center, one or two knots, as necessary, being made to hold them firmly. Take as many strands for each knotting as, from the width of the drawn space, you will be able to tie together without curving or hooping the material too much along the knot chain. There should be an even number for each cluster. Ten are used in the pattern illustrated. The more strands taken the more distinct will be the curved knotting of the design, which is its principle feature. If but a few strands are taken, the diamond-shaped spaces between the strands, instead of being broad, as they should be, will be very narrow, thus leaving no room for a well-defined curved knotting. Knot clusters of strands all along the center, as seen at No. 2, carrying the thread from one knotting to another. By referring to the completed design shown at No. 1, it will be seen that this knotting thread is *not* carried from one cluster to another *along the middle of the finish* at each side of the center. Each cluster is tied or knotted at the center, and the thread is then carried down an outer strand to the fabric and then still along the back of the work to the next cluster; here it is carried up an outer strand to the middle, where

NO. 3.—DETAIL FOR BORDER DESIGN.

the cluster is knotted, then down the same strand to the fabric, and so on all across the work.

The second step of the work may be seen again

at No. 3. After the clusters are all knotted, as seen at No. 2, the worker must decide how many distinct lines of knotting are to be made; and this estimate must be the same for each half of the design. If five are decided upon, as in No. 1, the two halves of the design will then each be divided into six equal parts. Now, one-sixth of the distance from the center to the knot chain begin the first knotting. When each cluster contains as many knottings as are here given, it is always well, when the first knotting comes so near the center, to tie *two* strands with *each* knot. The next knotting and the subsequent ones, however, take up but *one* strand at a time, and the knotting, which is really the knot chain, must be so graduated that the work will remain flat and the strands radiate like the sticks of a fan, while the knotting itself, instead of forming a straight outline, will extend in a slight curve which results from the strands being drawn tightly together at the center and spreading therefrom. When the knotting next to the center of the *first* cluster is made the cotton is carried to the *lower* portion of the *lower* half of the *second* cluster, and the knotting crosses it one-sixth of the distance from the knot chain along the edge to the center, each knot tying *one* strand. The cotton is then carried up to the upper half of the third cluster near the middle, and a knotting of double strands like the first one is made. These details are carried across the entire work, and the method of making the tyings is fully represented by the arrangement of the thread and needle pictured in the engraving.

All of the first set of lines of knotting are represented by No. 4, each being made by the method just described, except that but one strand at a time is taken up by each knot in all the lines except the first one made. The *first* two lines of

the *second* set of knottings, which cross the first ones in the diamond-shaped spaces, are also represented by No. 4. They are made precisely the same as the corresponding ones in the first set, crossing the strands in the same order; but where the lines intersect, knots are made in the diamond-shaped spaces. The arrangement of the needle and thread show how the knots are made where the lines also cross the middle thread; and this same movement is used in knotting the lines together at their other intersections. The remaining three lines of the *second* set of knottings are made the same as the corresponding ones of the *first* set, great care being taken to preserve the curve represented by the direction taken by the knottings.

An inspection of No. 1 will, after the center has been completed, at once make plain the arrangement of the finish at each side of the center. It has been explained in the foregoing details how the strands for the finish are knotted at the center, and the knotting thread is then carried down to the fabric and passed invisibly along the back of the work to the next cluster. Each cluster for the finish contains half the number of strands used for each center cluster, as will be seen by referring to the engraving; and each half of every cluster is divided into thirds by two sets of knottings, every knot of which ties but *one* strand. Having made the center, it will be perfectly easy for the learner to understand and make this part of the work.

While this is a difficult pattern in one sense, in another it is quite simple. It appears intricate, but is in reality very easy to follow, since the knottings are regularly made in each direction. The difficulty is mainly in making smooth work, but as before suggested, time and patience will develop the skill necessary to produce results so perfect that the worker will feel amply repaid for her efforts.

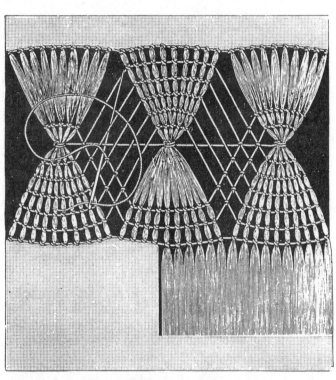

No. 4.—DETAIL FOR BORDER DESIGN.

CHAPTER VIII.

DESIGN IN DRAWN-WORK.

By this time our pupils are undoubtedly far enough advanced to develop the patterns given in succeeding articles without any special instruc-

a sufficient guide for their application in different designs. But for the benefit of those who prefer something to rely upon other than information

No. 1.—Design in Drawn-Work.

tions, for the knotting is the same in all the steps, and having once mastered these, the eye becomes

conveyed by the eye, we continue to present complete instructions for the details of each design.

DESIGN IN DRAWN-WORK.

No. 1.—This design is similar in some respects to the one shown in the preceding chapter and is developed, to a certain extent, in the same way. The knotting of the fan portions is identical, but the arrangement where the threads cross is quite different and is fully explained further on in this

No. 2.

spider, as it resembles both. A pretty variation may be made in the darning as follows: After the wheel or web is made, darn together separately each set of triple threads radiating from the wheel, as shown at No. 6. The result will be a sort of Maltese cross, and it may either entirely take the place of the pattern illustrated or may alternate with it or with the lattice-work crossings seen in the design in chapter VII.; or the wheel or web effect may be used in combination with the lattice-work. The narrow headings may also be made after any of the knotting designs previously given for the purpose, or the undrawn spaces may be left perfectly plain by knotting the strands at the edges of the fabric, as seen in the details. Undoubtedly learners who are fond of inventing little variations in the details of any fancy-work they may do will find even prettier ones than are herein suggested. The student is by no means compelled to exactly copy the design given unless it satisfies her artistic eyes and taste.

This design is suitable for any of the purposes heretofore mentioned and is very effective on any appropriate material.

DETAILS FOR DESIGN.

Nos. 2, 3 AND 4.—The first steps for making

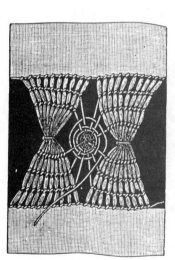

No. 3.

No. 4.

Nos. 2, 3 AND 4.—DETAILS FOR DESIGN.

article. There are three distinct rows of fans separated by a narrow heading, which is also illustrated in the present number. It will be observed that the fans are arranged so as to bring the diamond-shaped spaces of each row directly at the middle of the fans in the rows above and below. The wheel at the center of each space is sometimes called a spider's web and sometimes a

the fan portions are illustrated at No. 2. When the the threads have been drawn for the complete design, the fabric is placed in the frame, and the knotting of the strands is done either by the knot chain stitch, if the narrow spaces are to be plain, or by fancy knotting, if they are to represent headings. The knotting of the fan portions themselves is done after the manner described for the design before mentioned with this exception: In this pattern the threads are not knotted into a lattice-work in the spaces, but cross loosely or unknotted until the thread which makes the upper knotting at the top of the first fan is brought into the space; then this thread, by a single knot-stitch made exactly at the center of the space, draws all the other threads closely together. The engraving

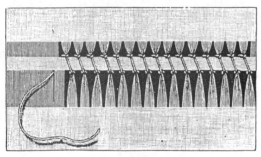

No. 5.

shows how the needle is inserted *under* the crossing threads and *over* the loop made by the top thread, to properly make the knotting. When the knot is drawn taut and the radiating threads are all smooth and even, darn under and over them, as shown at No. 3, until the wheel or web is as large as you want it. Then fasten it by the process illustrated at No. 4, and make the final knotting of the next fan. This knotting will be next to the center of the fan in every instance, but will be alternately above and below it. Three rows of knotting are made the full length of the work after the method given in chapter VII. The first two rows are made so that their threads will cross, as illustrated, in the spaces; and the thread of the last row knots the centers and forms the wheels. If desired, the thread which knots the strands together at the center to form each fan portion may be carried along the middle from one fan to the other, but the method illustrated, which was fully explained in the previous article, is the one generally preferred.

DETAILS FOR HEADING, AND MALTESE-CROSS DARNING.

Nos. 5 and 6.—The heading shown at No. 5 *is* easily done and is very effective. It is the first knotting made after the work is put in the frame, and the larger strands here shown are intended to correspond with those of the fan portions seen in the full design. The knotted threads of the narrow space are the same as those of the knotted strands, but by the arrangement of the thread they appear to extend between the strands of the fan. The *first* one of these strands is knotted in the usual manner; then the thread is carried obliquely *over* the narrow space to the top of the latter, where it knots the threads belonging to the *second* strand of the fan. The thread is then brought down vertically on the *under* side of the work to this *second* strand, which is then knotted, and the thread again carried obliquely to the threads of the *third* strand at the top of the space. If this work is correctly done, the thread will lie *obliquely* on the *right* side of the work and perpendicularly on the *wrong* side.

No. 6 shows the application of the heading, and

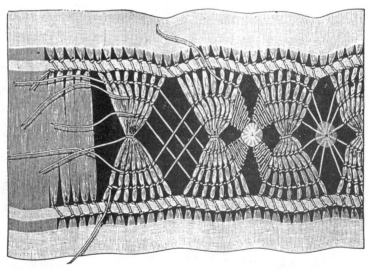

No. 6.

Nos. 5 and 6.—Details for Heading and Maltese-Cross Darning.

also how the Maltese-cross effect is obtained. As the student progressses she will be surprised to find how many pretty designs in darning she will be able to develop from her own creative genius. The design represented by No. 6 may be applied just as it is—that is, only the one row and heading—to tidies, scarfs and any article of personal or household linen to which such work is suited.

CHAPTER IX.
DESIGN IN DRAWN-WORK.

DESIGN IN DRAWN-WORK.

No. 1.—The design represented in full by this

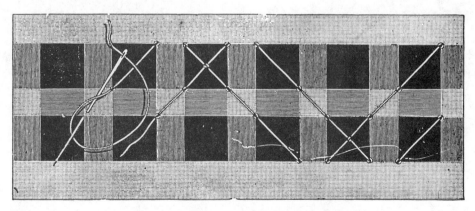

NO. 1.—DESIGN IN DRAWN-WORK.

children's dresses, and for undergarments, aprons, scarfs and tidies; and the material may be fine or coarse linen, pongee or any fabric the threads of which may be successfully drawn for such work. Only one row of stars is here shown, but, as will be seen by referring to No. 6, two or as many rows as may be desired may be made by following the directions given for the details pictured at Nos. 4 and 5. The heading may be added at either side of a number of rows in precisely the same manner as is here illustrated; or any of the headings previously given may be substituted; or, if a heading is not desired, the center portion of the design may be made as shown at No. 6. In the pattern from which this design was taken the narrow strip of fabric at its lower edge is a hem, and it may be made of the width indicated or of that seen at No. 6, where a corner is turned over to show the method of procedure. The narrow hem, however, is made on the under side of the fabric, while the wider one is turned over on the upper side. Lace or fringe may be added to this hem, according to the nature of the article decorated by the design. A wide hem below this border with a tuck above, would form a pretty combination. Or, a hem,

NO. 2.—DETAIL FOR DESIGN.

engraving may be developed particularly well with fine linen or linen lawn as foundation material. It is especially appropriate for the skirts of ladies' and children's dresses, and for undergarments, aprons,

a cluster of tucks, then the border and another cluster would be a dainty finish for a child's dress or petticoat or an infant's robe.

3

DETAILS FOR DESIGN.

Nos. 2, 3, 4, 5, 6 and 7.—The first thing to be done in beginning this design is to decide upon the size of the squares, and then draw the threads. At No. 2, page 15, the plan for drawing and cutting secure the cut edges by a close over-and-over stitch working from left to right. The effect of this finish when closely made will be that of a cord. A button-hole or chain stitch may be used instead of the over-and-over finish; but this is not applied until the pattern is completed. The over-and-

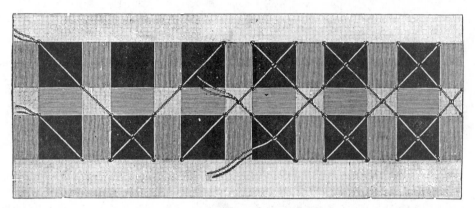

No. 3.—Detail for Design.

threads in very similar squares is illustrated and described, the only difference being that in this instance *more threads are drawn* in order to make square *spaces*, instead of *solid squares* as seen in the detail mentioned. As perfect squares are desired, the number of threads drawn in each direction will depend entirely upon the nature of the fabric. In some cases the threads of the warp and filling will be about even in size, while in others they will vary. When they are not even, the best plan will be to measure off the squares and the spaces from which the threads are to be drawn, and in that over finish has not been represented, as the button-hole or chain stitch might be considered preferable, while the illustration of either one stitch or the other might cause the learner to infer that no other was suitable.

At No. 2 on the preceding page, only the spaces for the center portion of the design have been given; but in preparing the material for the completed design the threads must also be drawn for the heading, leaving the narrow solid strip at each side to be crossed by the stitches used in knotting the strands of the headings; and these stitches may

No. 4.

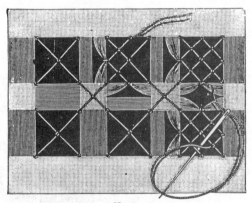

No. 5.

Nos. 4 and 5.—Details for Design.

way regulate the number. When the squares are measured and marked, cut across the top and bottom of each square that is to be drawn with a pair of fine, sharp scissors or a very sharp penknife, and then remove the lengthwise threads as shown at No. 2, page 15. When all the squares are drawn, also stay the edges of the fabric where the threads are cut out of the square spaces.

Having drawn all the threads, put the fabric into the frame, and then commence the knotting. Begin the first thread at the upper right corner of the upper right open square or space; carry it diagonally down to the small solid square, knotting it at each corner; and then cross the *second* lower space the same as the first one crossed, knotting the thread at its lower left corner. Then pass the thread *under* the strand now next it; and knot it at the lower right corner of the third lower space,

NO. 6.—DETAIL FOR DESIGN.

also at each of the two corners of the next small solid square, as seen in the engraving, and finally at the upper left corner of the fourth open square in the upper row. Repeat this process the full length of the work, making the knots as shown by the needle and loop in the engraving. Then begin the second knotting thread at the upper right corner of the first open square in the lower row, and apply the principles of the directions just given, crossing each open and solid square obliquely, and making the knottings at the corners, and also at the *crossings of the threads*, as seen in the illustration. When these two threads are carried across the work, then, with two others—one at a time—begun at the *lower* right corners of the first squares, go over all the spaces in the work in the same way as before, except that when the threads are crossed and knotted over the solid blocks the knotting stitch is taken through the fabric. No. 3 fully illustrates the work at this point of its development.

Up to this time four knotting threads have been used. Now begin a fifth (see No. 4), knotting half the threads in the strand between the first upper and lower spaces; carry the thread up to the first diagonal thread to the left (see method in the *second* upper square), and knot it as shown by the needle and loop in the *second* square. Next take up half the *second* upright strand, knotting it at

the middle; then carry the thread to the right, knotting it at its crossing with the diagonal one; knot it again at the middle of the top of the space, then at the next diagonal crossing to the right; and then knot the adjoining half of the *first* upright strand, carry the thread to the left and knot the next diagonal thread, and finally slip the needle through the first knot made in the crosswise strand, bringing the thread to the under side of the work. This completes the filling in of the first space in the upper row.

Now bring the thread along at the back of the work to the middle of the second horizontal strand; knot half of this strand as seen at No. 4, and proceed as in the first space. The second space shows how the first knotting of every diagonal crossing is made; and the *second* space in No. 5 shows accurately how the work proceeds, just as described. No. 5 also illustrates the *first* space of the lower row filled in, and where the last knotting of every space is performed and just how the knot is tied.

No. 6 shows how *three* rows of spaces will look when filled in, and also how a hem may be turned up on the outside and fastened by the ordinary process, which will at the same time secure the raw edges of the open spaces. Of course, this hem should be made before the spaces are filled in with the knotted threads.

No. 7 shows how the main portion of the heading is made. By referring to No. 1 it will be seen that the strands of the upper heading are separated at their tops by the knot chain, and at the opposite side by the thread being knotted from side to side over the narrow strip, just as has been described and illustrated on several previous occasions. At the bottom of the work the same method is em-

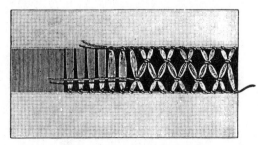

NO. 7.—DETAIL FOR DESIGN.

ployed to separate the strands, except that the tiny hem is caught to place by the knotting. The method of knotting the strands together for the heading is clearly explained by the engraving and needs no further description. This heading may be replaced by any other preferred or hitherto presented.

CHAPTER X.

DESIGN FOR DRAWN-WORK.

A pattern similar in some of its details to those illustrated at No. 1 in chapter VIII, and No. 1 in chapter IX, is here presented. The design, like a number of those which have preceded it, will be found appropriate for skirts, dresses, aprons, scarfs, tidies, etc.; and any of the fabrics heretofore mentioned may be used for its successful development.

The latter may be varied according to the individual taste of the student, who may substitute other given or

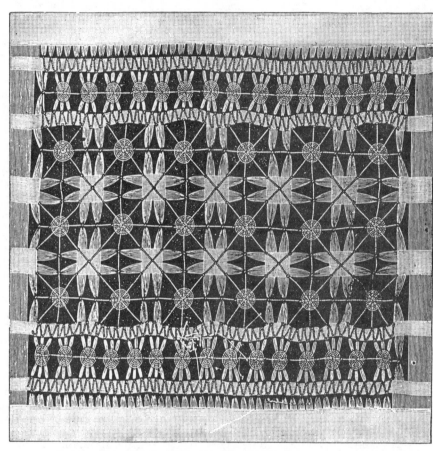

No. 1.—Design for Drawn-Work.

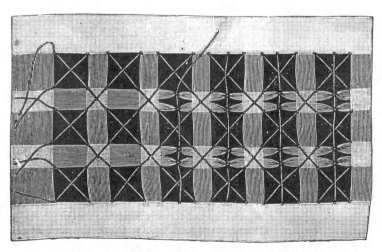

No. 2.—Detail for Design.

original borders for those at each side of the design, or omit them altogether.

DESIGN FOR DRAWN-WORK.

No. 1.—This engraving illustrates a completed design and shows how the threads are to be drawn for the headings after all the other threads have been drawn for the main portion of the pattern. As many rows of stars and spider webs as may be desired may be made before the headings are added; and any other of the headings previously described may be substituted for the one illustrated, although the latter is in perfect keeping with the remainder of the border or design. If it is desirable, in making the design for a skirt, to have it cross breadths from side to side after the manner of tucks or embroidery, instead of following a selvedge, the threads may be so drawn that one-half the strands for a star

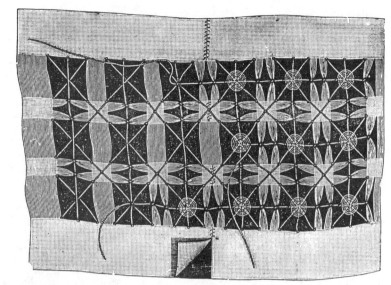

No. 3.

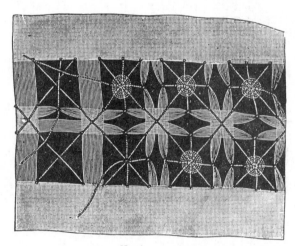

No. 4.

Nos 3 and 4.—Details for Design.

will come out as wanted; and this may be done by slightly increasing or decreasing the threads of the strands, as may be required, in order to bring them out in such a manner that the strands for one-half of a star will come at the selvedge. A little practice in this respect will enable the learner to produce a satisfactory result without difficulty.

DETAILS FOR DESIGN.

Nos. 2, 3 and 4.—The method of drawing and clipping the threads has been explained in the preceding chapter. The diagonal knottings are made precisely as those in the design mentioned,

will take up a selvedge at each side of every breadth; and adjoining breadths may then be sewed together at each little solid square before the knotting begins, so that the joining will be scarcely perceptible. By referring to No. 3 at the point where a corner is turned over, the worker may observe how such a joining is made. It may be necessary, when nearing a selvedge, to so calculate that the strands

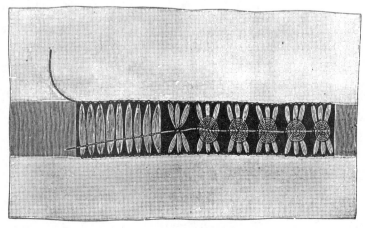

No. 5.—Finish for Design.

except that they are not tied where they cross at the middle of each space. When all the open spaces have been crossed without knotting, and all the small squares crossed and knotted, as seen in the engraving, begin a thread at the middle of the top of a space and bring it down vertically to the first horizontal strand of drawn threads; take up half of this strand, and knot it as shown in the engraving; then, after a short allowance of the knotting thread or cotton, take up the other half of the strand and knot it in a similar manner. After this the next space is crossed and the next lower strand knotted in the same manner as the upper one; and finally the cotton is carried across the lower or last space and fastened at the middle of its lower edge. Every space is crossed by a vertical thread knotted as described, and then a horizontal knotting is begun (see No. 4), and continued as follows : Knot the inner half of the first upper upright strand, carry the thread to the center of the space, and there knot all the meeting and crossing threads with it; then weave the needle over and under the radiating threads to make a spider or spider web, as described in chapter VIII. When the spider or web is large enough, finish it with a knot made exactly opposite the beginning of this thread, and carry the latter to the next upright strand, knotting one-half of it. Make a short allowance, the same as in the vertical knotting, carry it back of the strands as suggested further on, and then knot the other half of the strand. Carry the thread to the center of the next space and proceed to make another spider or web the same as before. Complete each row of strands and spaces in a similar manner. A close inspection of the engravings will show how every step of the details is carried out, from knotting the crossing threads to finishing the spider. The crossing threads must be very accurately allowed in

order to give the finished work a smooth effect.

No. 4 also shows how the "short allowance" may be omitted in effect, by passing the cotton to the back of the work after knotting the first half of the strand, and then bringing it out at the knotting of the second half, thus leaving the space between the strands perfectly open. The effect will then be more lace-like.

When drawing near the end of a needleful of working cotton, stop using it where you knot all the threads together. Then take a new cotton, draw it up through the knot, and weave the short end of the first cotton in and out with the new one in making the spider. This plan will obviate the necessity of making a joining of the threads, which would be more or less clumsy.

FINISH FOR DESIGN.

No. 5.—This engraving fully explains itself. After the strands are separated in the usual manner, they are knotted together in sets of three. As each set is knotted it is also darned or woven in and out in spider fashion, and the spider is finished with a knot before the next three strands are knotted. The little heading observed at each side of the finish at No. 1 may be omitted, if not desired, but it is a dainty addition and requires but little more work. It is quite a matter of necessity between the design and the finish; but between the latter and the plain fabric it may be left out.

Regarding the introduction of color by using variously tinted working cottons, the suggestions we have offered on previous occasions still hold good. All-white work is daintier and more refined, but there are some fancy articles which may be made more showy by the use of colored cottons. The selection of the latter is, of course, purely a matter of taste.

CHAPTER XI.

DESIGN FOR DRAWN-WORK.

It is quite needless to suggest the various uses to which this pretty design is adapted. Like its predecessors, it may be applied to a variety of articles how many rows deep she wishes the points of the pattern to be and draw the threads accordingly. For purposes of illustrating and explaining the de-

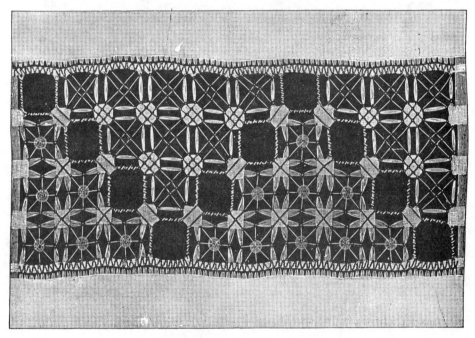

No. 1.—DESIGN FOR DRAWN-WORK.

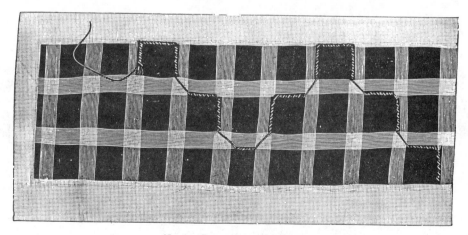

No. 2. — DETAIL FOR THE POINTS.

and developed in any of the numerous fabrics heretofore indicated and suggested.

In preparing the fabric the worker must decide tails but three rows of spaces (see No. 9) have been given, but in the completed design four rows appear, with a very effective result.

DESIGN FOR DRAWN-WORK.

No. 1.—By closely studying this illustration in the open spaces mark out a set of points whose squares are filled in by two distinct patterns, one of which, the star pattern, was given in chapter

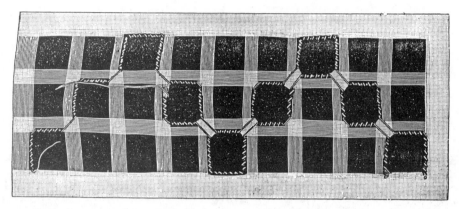

No. 3.—Detail for the Points.

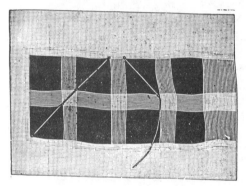

No. 4.

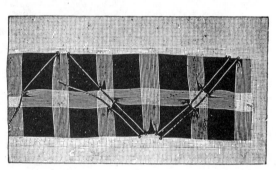

No. 5.

No. 6.

No. 7.

Nos. 4, 5, 6 and 7.—Details for Filling In Design.

connection with the engravings of the details, the student will be able to produce the design unaided by explicit instructions. It will be observed that X., while the details for the other are included in this article. Of course, it will not be necessary to include the two patterns in filling in the spaces, but the two combined make a prettier effect than one alone.

DETAILS FOR THE POINTS.

Nos. 2 AND 3.—These engravings show how the threads are to be drawn and cut by the method described in previous chapters. All the raw edges about the spaces are finished with a close over-

No. 8.—DETAIL FOR FILLING IN DESIGN.

and-over stitch to prevent ravelling, after which the points are begun as seen at the lower right corner of No. 2. One-half of this upright strand of threads is wound round and round, producing a cord effect; and the same winding is continued around the lower half of the first horizontal strand reached. The thread is then carried diagonally across the corner of the adjoining small solid square to the beginning of the second upright strand, the inner half of which is wound the same as the first one; then one-half the adjoining horizontal strand is wound, the next small square is diagonally crossed, and the inner half of the third upright strand is wound. The edge of the third upper space is now reached, and by an over-and-over stitch the cord effect is continued across it to the fourth upright strand. The right half of the strand is wound and then the lower half of the adjoining horizontal strand; and this process is carried out, always in a diagonal direction, either upward or downward until the work is crossed.

By comparing Nos. 2 and 3, it will be seen that at No. 2 the winding process takes in only *two* of the sets of horizontal strands. The same is also true of the second cotton or thread, which is begun at the right half of the second upright strand of the lowest row in No. 3; but the two cottons complete the points and the wound strands so that all three of the horizontal strands are taken up as the work progresses.

DETAILS FOR FILLING IN DESIGN.

Nos. 4, 5, 6, 7, 8 AND 9.—Details for filling in the star pattern were given in the preceding chapter, and as the learner is no doubt familiar with them, it will not be necessary to give them further mention, since No. 3 shows exactly where and how they are to be applied. The engravings whose numbers have just been given fully illustrate, step by step, the method of filling in those spaces wherein the star pattern is not used. Four working cottons cross each space, and where they cross at the center they are knotted; and at each corner of every small solid square they each knot a strand. The worker must be very careful to knot the proper strand each time, for a slight mistake in the beginning will spoil the whole work. It is therefore advisable that she begin and carry out one cotton at a time as seen at No. 4; then begin and follow with the second as seen at No. 5. This done, the other two cottons may be begun as seen at No. 6; while additional ones complete Nos. 7 and 8. It will be observed that where the cottons cross over the small squares they are knotted, but not *to* the square as in the star pattern. All these knottings make a very lace-like effect, but they must be regularly and neatly made. The di-

No. 9.—DETAIL FOR FILLING IN DESIGN.

rections just given may be easily adapted to the spaces within the points, if the student will carefully inspect the design as represented at No. 1. In fact, with all the knowledge on the subject she is now in posession of, the worker may find the engraving a more valuable assistant than a lengthy word description.

The design is completed by a tiny heading which has been represented and described a number of times; therefore no difficulty will be experienced in making it.

CHAPTER XII.

DESIGN FOR A BORDER IN DRAWN-WORK.

The design here illustrated and described differs essentially from any of its predecessors. It is worked in one direction by means of the knot chain and a button-hole stitch, and the knotting of the strands occurs as the first row of the work proceeds, instead of being done separately as a pre-

found in the making of the stitches evenly and the carrying of the working cotton in straight parallel lines between the button-hole work. Perfect regularity in both respects must be observed, or the work will surely prove a failure. An important item to be considered is the preparation of the

No. 1.—Design for a Border in Drawn-Work.

liminary detail. This pattern is very handsome for pillow and bolster slips, sheets, towels, tidies or any article requiring a border, being in effect not unlike the pillow-slip lace so fashionable in our grandmothers' days. The only difficulties that will be encountered in reproducing the design will be

space to be worked. All the threads must not be drawn at once, but one-half or two-thirds of them may be drawn after the width of the decoration has been decided upon. The reason for this is that the exact depth required cannot be estimated, and upon completing the last row of stitches in the order of the progression it might be found that too many threads had been drawn, so that the labor thus far spent would be lost. If, however,

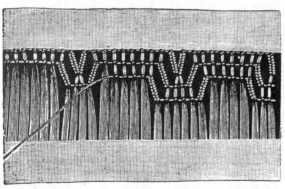

No. 2.

about one-half or two-thirds of the threads are drawn, the worker can, toward the completion of the border, draw as many more as the pattern requires and thus terminates the work properly.

DESIGN FOR A BORDER IN DRAWN-WORK.

No. 1.—This engraving shows the border with a supplementary finish at each side made by the "duck's-trail" stitch described in chapter

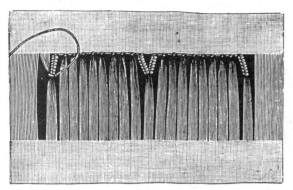

No. 4.

II. This finish, however, may be omitted, and any of the headings previously described may be substituted for it. For tidies, bureau-scarfs or any article permitting the introduction of color, working cottons of various tints may be used instead of the white; or, if white working cotton is used, the design may be neatly under-laid with a daintily-tinted ribbon or with strips of colored silk, satin, sateen, foulard or Silesia, with a very satisfactory and pretty result.

DETAILS FOR BORDER IN DRAWN-WORK.

Nos. 2, 3, 4, 5, 6 AND 7.—The progression of the work necessary to the development of the border shown at No. 1 is clearly illustrated by successive engravings. No. 2 pictures the first step after the drawing of a portion of the threads. A strand is taken up by a row of button-hole stitches made along it from the first (lowest) stitch to the edge of the fabric

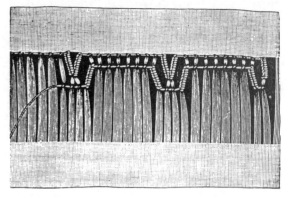

No. 3.

above; then nine other strands are divided off by the knot chain, making ten strands now knotted, counting the button-hole stitched strand first formed. Make a series of button-hole stitches down the tenth strand to correspond in number and effect with those on the first strand, working downward. If a larger pattern is wanted, more strands must be knotted between the button-holed strands; but they must always be of an even number. It is best, also, to count the button-hole stitches for each strand until the eye becomes accustomed to making them uniform in number.

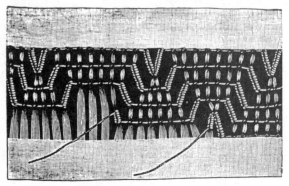

No. 5.

Nos. 2, 3, 4 AND 5.—DETAILS FOR BORDER IN DRAWN-WORK.

When the last button-hole stitch on the tenth strand has been made, join another (the eleventh) unknotted strand to the tenth at the lowest stitch by the usual knot stitch; then button-hole stitch this strand upward to the fabric, and knot nine more strands, procceding as before and as shown

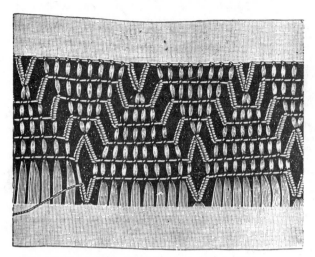

No. 6.—DETAIL FOR BORDER IN DRAWN-WORK.

by the illustration. Continue in this manner entirely across the work for the first row.

No. 3 shows how the second row of the work is made. The details are the same in principle as those of the first row, but the strands are differently connected. The first strand of the first row is knotted to the first strand of the second row a little below the first button-hole stitch made, and then the same number of button-hole stitches are made, working upward. After the uppermost stitch is made the thread is carried in a horizontal line to the next strand and a knot stitch is made; the next six strands are similarly knotted, after which the button-hole stitches are made down the last knotted strand to correspond with those on the first strand of the second row. After the last button-hole stitch is made, the thread is again carried to the left; and the two strands that are joined together above are now *knotted separately*. The next strand is also knotted as seen in the illustration, and is then ascended by the uniform number of button-hole stitches, after which all the knotting of the second row just described is repeated until the whole work is crossed.

No. 4 illustrates how the third row is begun and carried along, and it can be followed without difficulty, since the other two rows have been so accurately described. Care must be taken to have all the button-hole stitches lie in the same direction

—that is, with their edges turning toward the left.

No. 5 represents two more rows begun, and also shows where the work may stop for a narrow pattern displaying half diamonds or points. It also represents half of the design illustrated by No. 1.

Nos. 6 and 7 clearly illustrate how the subsequent rows necessary to fully complete the pattern are begun and carried on. If the worker takes each row by itself and follows it carefully according to the engraving, she will have no trouble in easily developing the full design, and as she approaches its completion she will more clearly understand the reason for drawing only part of the threads at a time.

This pattern may be varied in effect in two or three ways. For instance, the working cotton selected may be as thick as a strand, and the button-hole stitches may be sufficient in number to make the spaces between the knottings *perfect squares*, instead of oblongs, as here represented; or, a small number of strands may be tied by the knot chain— say four or six—between the button-holed strands, and the latter may have their stitches extended to a greater depth or number, thus producing small and slender figures.

Individual taste and ingenuity will find ample opportunity for exercise in this design, which is one of the most practical of the series here illus-

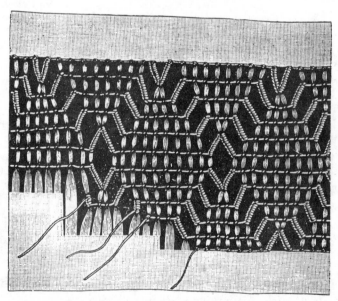

No. 7.—DETAIL FOR BORDER IN DRAWN-WORK.

trated, inasmuch as it is strong, easy to follow, attractive to the eye and adaptable to countless articles of personal or household use.

CHAPTER XIII.

BORDER DESIGN IN DRAWN-WORK.

The present design is one of great delicacy and beauty, but inasmuch as it involves many of the principles illustrated in previous chapters, the

No. 1.—BORDER DESIGN IN DRAWN-WORK.

skilled worker should experience little difficulty in reproducing it. The student who has not mastered all the intricacies of the patterns heretofore given, but who has a fair knowledge of foundation stitches, etc., will also be able, by the following instructions and a careful inspection of the accompanying illustrations, to copy the design with little or no trouble.

BORDER DESIGN IN DRAWN-WORK.

No. 1.—This handsome design may be used for the decoration of handkerchiefs, scarfs, tidies, towels, babies' dresses and petticoats, and large and small fancy aprons; and it may be suitably worked upon coarse or fine linen, pongee and China silk. It will be observed that the hemstitch effect along the outer edges of the finish is similar to that seen at No. 5 in chapter VIII., where it is more fully explained than in the present instance. When

threads have been drawn as disclosed by the design, the narrow spaces are separated at the edges of the material into tiny strands by the knot chain, after which they are again knotted, and at the same time the knotting thread is carried across the narrow strip of the material to knot the strands on the other side of it, the two knottings being done alternately. By this process the narrower strip is crossed *diagonally* by the knotting thread on the outside and *perpendicularly* on the under side. The wider heading is knotted on the same principle as that which will be explained in the details given below; but the knotting of the strands at its inner edges, in connection with those of the border itself, is the same as that just described for the hemstitch effect. For the latter the thread used should be finer than that forming the knotted crossed lines in the main portion of the border, and when a hem is used below the entire border, the hemstitching at the top of the border should be done on the same side as that on which the hem is made. In chapter II. the various methods of hemming were fully described, and it will not be necessary to repeat their details here.

DETAILS FOR THE CENTER OF THE BORDER.

Nos. 2, 3, 4 AND 5.—In beginning this design, the first thing to be done is to draw the threads; and in this design, as indeed, in most others,

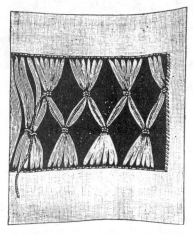

No. 2.—DETAIL FOR THE CENTER OF THE BORDER.

it is well to leave a small section of material at the end at which you begin (and also at the other end), as illustrated at the right-hand edges of the detail engravings. Before beginning to draw the threads, measure off the desired width of the design, and with a sharp knife or a pair of scissors make a slash the width of the design and half an inch from the selvedge or lengthwise edge of the goods; then draw the threads from this slash to a corresponding one at the other side of the fabric or article. Closely over-hand or button-hole stitch the edges, as shown in the engravings, to form a secure foundation upon which to begin working.

The first steps of the details are illustrated at No. 2. The drawn space is separated into strands by the knot-chain stitch in the usual manner. The fans are next knotted and must consist of an even number of strands, six being shown in this instance and ten at No. 1. To plainly illustrate the necessity for an even number, take up the first detail, pictured at No. 2. First draw half a fan, or three strands, to the button-holed edge, and fasten it firmly a-third of the distance from the knot chain at one edge; then carry

No. 3.

the same principle as that illustrated and explained by the details of the design in chapter VII., and is also clearly pictured in the present engraving, which shows how to begin and how and where to carry the thread. It will be observed that the thread is not only knotted about the separate strands of each fan, but also about the bars between the fans, in order to give a clearness to the design and strength to the work. As explained in previous articles treating of other similar designs, the first knotting thread may pass about each separate strand next to where a fan is tied or knotted; but if the fabric is very fine, and many strands must, in consequence, be tied in each fan, then two or three strands may be tied by the first knotting thread; and as the other knotting threads are added and the strands spread out they may be knotted individually. This point, it will be remembered, has been thoroughly explained and illustrated in preceeding articles.

The first thread to cross and knot to all of the

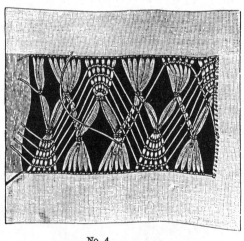

No. 4.

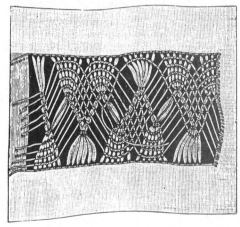

No. 5.

NOS. 3, 4 AND 5.—DETAILS FOR THE CENTER OF THE BORDER.

the knotting thread down another third of the space, and with one or two knots, as may be needed, tie six strands, or a whole fan, together. Carry the thread along the three strands at the left half of this fan to within a third of the distance from the upper edge, and there knot three more strands with the three just mentioned, to form the second whole fan. Proceed in this way, as illustrated, across the entire drawn space, to provide a foundation for the knotting.

No. 3 shows the first steps completed and the cross-knotting begun. The knotting is done on

first set of threads is illustrated at No. 4, and the engraving fully shows the method, which should be familiar by now to most of our readers.

At No. 5 the first thread of the last set of knotting threads is shown, and both it and all the others are knotted in the manner illustrated. When the knotting is completed the effect is very delicate and lace-like.

It is not necessary to use the finish seen at each side of the border; any of the other headings previously given may be substituted, if preferred.

CHAPTER XIV.

BORDER DESIGNS IN DRAWN-WORK.

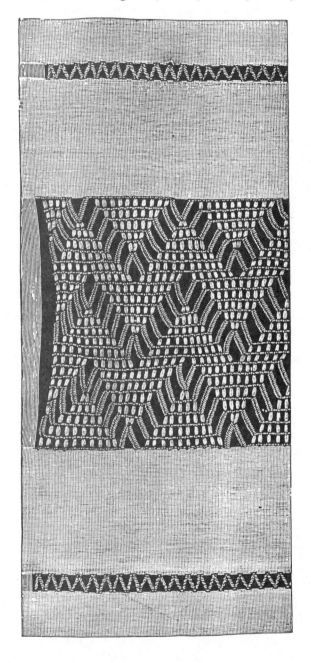

NO. 1.—DESIGN FOR A BORDER.

NO. 2.—BORDER DESIGN.

Owing to the great popularity of designs like that represented in chapter XII we illustrate in the present lesson three pretty specimens of the same class.   The details for this style of knotting were given step by step in the chapter mentioned; and as the principles there involved are perfectly applicable to the patterns now under consideration, we do not deem it necessary to enter into detail, but would refer such of our readers as have not already mastered this method of knotting to the chapter just mentioned for full instructions. Any of these designs may be employed in the decoration of table-cloths, bed linen, bureau and buffet scarfs, towels, aprons, children's skirts and dresses and ladies underwear. Done in heavy linen the effect is rich and artistic; and when the finer varieties of linen or of any of the dainty silken fabrics, such as pongee, are used, the work has delicate, lace-like appearance that is extremely desirable. No matter what fabric is selected, however, unless the knotting is done with care and precision, the result is certain to be disappointing.

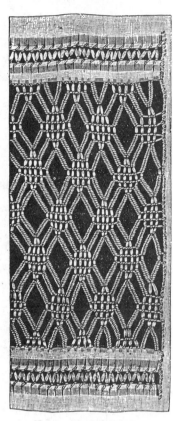

NO. 3.—BORDER DESIGN.

DESIGN FOR A BORDER.

No. 1.—If preferred, this design may be used without the narrow heading at each side; or it may be made above a hemstitched hem or be used above or below a deep finish like that seen at No. 2. Individual taste will, of course, direct its application in conjunction with any of the other designs heretofore given; for when the learner becomes expert in the work, her inventive genius usually asserts itself and she unites and varies the patterns already mastered, thus producing, in many instances, charming and original effects.

The method of making the narrow heading is fully illustrated at No. 4. The heading is divided

by knotting, into the strands seen at No. 5, each strand being wound after every knotting.

BORDER DESIGN.

No. 2.—Owing to lack of space we are unable to fully picture the fabric upon which this design is worked; that being the case, we have reversed the design—that is, in the original design the main work appeared between a deep hemstitched hem and the broad, fancy finish seen below the main work in the engraving. The narrow line above the main work in the engraving is really the hemstitching that confines the hem in the sample from which the illustration was made. That we were able to effectively reverse the pattern proves that the student may also depart from the original intention of the design in applying the latter to the fabric. But if she desires to use it as planned, the article to be decorated, if of coarse linen, must first be finished with a hemstitched hem two inches and a-half deep; then the main border must be made, and after this the rest of the work will be done, details being given at Nos. 5 and 6. These engravings, like No. 4, so clearly illustrate the method of the work that further description is not needed.

BORDER DESIGN.

No. 3.—This design, as originally developed, was done on fine but not sheer linen, but such as would be used for pillow-shams, table-scarfs, a child's dress or a plain apron. It is particularly effective on account of its open character, which produces an appearance similar to that of the meshes in lace. It may be made wide or narrow, and used either with or without the dainty finish at each side, which is again clearly illustrated at No. 5. The suggestions regarding

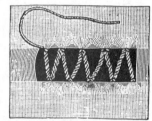

No. 4.

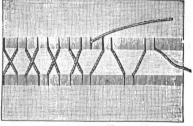

No. 5.

No. 6.

NOS. 4, 5 AND 6.—DETAILS FOR DESIGNS.

combinations offered in the descriptions of the two preceding designs apply equally well to this one.

CHAPTER XV.

BORDER DESIGNS IN DRAWN-WORK.

BORDER DESIGNS IN DRAWN-WORK.

Nos. 1 AND 2.—Two very handsome designs, intended for borders to skirts, aprons, dresses, tidies, scarfs, draperies, etc., etc., are illustrated by these engravings. Concerning the finish seen at

No. 1.—BORDER DESIGN IN DRAWN-WORK.

each side of each design very little need be said, as it is perfectly familiar to our students, and either can be easily copied by a beginner in drawn-work. Those desiring assistance, however, in developing them, will find detailed instructions on previous pages of this book.

The central portions of these two designs are

4

combinations of the details shown on the next page; No. 1 also including another variation which forms the foundation for the rest of the work. This variation consists of dividing each strand into thirds and then darning over and under the divisions as seen in the engraving, except at regular intervals, where the strands are separated as seen at No. 2. These exceptions may be arranged to please the taste of the worker, and wherever they are to occur, the knotting represented at No. 3 must first be made; but at the remaining squares this knotting will not be necessary. When all the strands are knotted and darned as seen in the engraving, the open squares are filled in by "spiders" or rosettes made after the methods heretofore described, and which are here made perfectly plain to any one who examines the engraving.

No. 2.—BORDER DESIGN IN DRAWN-WORK.

At No. 2 the squares are knotted into circles by the method which will be described at No. 3. The knotting between the strands is that which is also illustrated as a detail at Nos. 5 and 7; but the strands themselves are each divided into three parts, and this renders the work extremely delicate and lace-like in effect when the material is fine lawn. Nos. 1 and 2 are both especially adapted to fine fabrics. No. 1 is represented in full size and is done upon fine, closely woven linen. No. 2 is pictured half as large again as the fine lawn sample from which the engraving was made.

DETAILS FOR BORDER DESIGNS.

Nos. 3, 4, 5, 6 AND 7.—The details shown on

this page have been enlarged from the samples they represent so that the worker may encounter no difficulty whatever in following them.

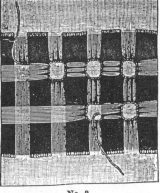

No. 8.

When the threads have been drawn and the strands are ready for knotting, button-hole all the raw edges to keep them from fraying out. Then, to make the solid squares into

In No. 4, having formed the first little circle, knot one-half of the horizontal strands between two circles exactly in the middle; then one-half of the vertical ones to the left, then one-half of the horizontal ones directly above, and lastly one-half of the ones to the right; bring the cotton down and knot or fasten it at the knot made around the first horizontal strands. Carry the cotton to the next solid square and proceed as before, first knotting the square into a circle. Work each row in the same manner.

No. 5 is No. 4 carried one step further. Omit the final knot of No. 4 and proceed to twist the working cotton around the little diamond design, as shown in the picture. When around the design then make the final knot, and then pass on to the next solid square. Work line by line until the design is all filled in. It is generally best to work the filling-in from left to right, though it does not make any very material difference in the result.

No. 6 somewhat resembles in the filling-in No. 4, but an inspection of the engraving will show that the cotton is *looped*, not *knotted*, around the strands. After the last loop is made the cotton is carried along the back of the work to the center of the next square, and the tiny embroidered dot is made.

No. 7 shows the filling-in seen at No. 5, with no knotting at, or decoration of, the squares, the threads of which are so drawn apart by the filling-in that a tiny open space is formed where each solid square is located in the other details.

No. 4

No. 5.

circles, knot the strands at each side as seen at No. 3, beginning at the right-hand side or upper corner of the first square. Work across the top of the little square, knotting the strands one by one, then down the left side, across the lower edge and up to the beginning; here draw the first and last knots together, take an invisible stitch (around a single thread) at the back of the circle now formed, and then carry the knotting cotton along the back of the work to the next square to the left, and proceed as in the first square. Work each row the same.

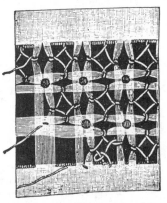

No. 6.

No. 7.

NOS. 3, 4, 5, 6 AND 7.—DETAILS FOR BORDER DESIGNS.

Any one of these details is exceedingly pretty for handkerchiefs, infants' shirts, doilies or any article to be made of very fine fabric.

CHAPTER XVI.
DESIGNS FOR BORDERS AND HEADINGS.

DESIGNS FOR BORDERS AND HEADINGS.

Nos. 1, 2, 3, 4, 5 AND 6.—These engravings show a variety of methods for bordering table linen, scarfs, towels, etc., etc., above an edge-finish composed of fringe or a hem.

No. 1 is knotted in a simple design with silk, which produces a very rich effect, and is appropriate for tray-cloths, carvers' cloths, towels or scarfs.

All of the other specimens are knotted with cotton or linen after the methods plainly indicated. The Grecian pattern above the open-work at No. 4 may be easily made from the picture; and the similar patterns between the two rows of open-work seen at No. 6 is first made like that at No. 4, and then a second thread is twisted around

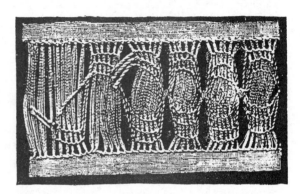

No. 1.

No. 2.

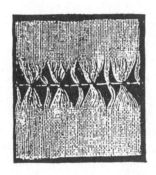

No. 3.

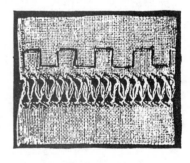

No. 4.

No. 5.

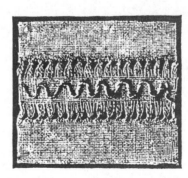

No. 6.

NOS. 1, 2, 3, 4, 5 AND 6.—DESIGNS FOR BORDERS AND HEADINGS.

the first one — over-and-under — entirely across the work; this produces the curves seen in the picture.

If desired color may be introduced into borders and headings like these, by using red or blue knotting cotton; or in Nos. 4 and 6, by using the colored cotton for the outline work only.

When only a hem is to be used in connection with either of these headings, it may be secured by the lower row of knotting in the heading chosen.

DESIGNS FOR NARROW BORDERS.

Nos. 7, 8 and 9.—These engravings illustrate three pretty methods of making simple borders and finishes for scarfs, curtains, tidies, table-spreads, napkins, doilies, etc. At No. 7 the knot chain is used to tie the strands at the middle, after which an extra cotton is twisted around the knotting thread between the strands, as seen in the engraving. The ornamental stitching above is familiar to every one as the cat-stitch, and is made from left to right, an upper stitch being taken, then a lower one, then an upper one, and so on across the work.

A hemstitched hem constitutes the edge finish of the design seen at No. 8 and is made in the usual

No. 7.

fringed towels, tidies, napkins, scarfs, doilies, etc. It is also seen along the edges of scrim window-curtains that are to be finished with hems alone or with hems and lace borders, and is used in making a plain finish on babies' skirts and along the lower edges of linen or scrim aprons.

The engraving at No. 9 shows a method of finish very popular for fancy articles made of canvas, butcher's linen and scrim, and also much used for napery. As represented, the cross-stitch, which is done with Saxony yarn upon canvas, is made across the entire article and then the threads are drawn, after which the strands are separated and drawn into the position seen by running a thread of the yarn "over and under" alternating groups of *four* threads

No. 8.

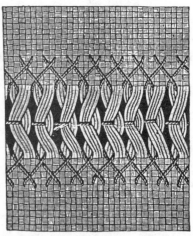

No. 9.

Nos. 7, 8 and 9.—Designs for Narrow Borders.

manner. The strands of the border above the hem may be easily knotted without instructions if the engraving is closely inspected. After each knot is made the cotton is twisted around half of the strand knotted and then carried to the next point to be knotted. It will be observed that the strands are divided so that those along the two edges alternate, the strands along the one edge coming between those of the other. This finish is popular for

each of the fabric. Sometimes this border is made wide enough to permit the use of a narrow ribbon for the separation of the strands; and then a deep, ravelled fringe of the fabric appears below the border. A handsome dust-cloth bag of unbleached canvas was decorated with such a border and fringe, the ribbon being nearly an inch wide and of a beautiful golden-green shade. If the cross-stitch is not desired, the strands may be stayed by fine overcasting.

CHAPTER XVII.

DESIGN FOR A LACE BORDER IN DRAWN-WORK.

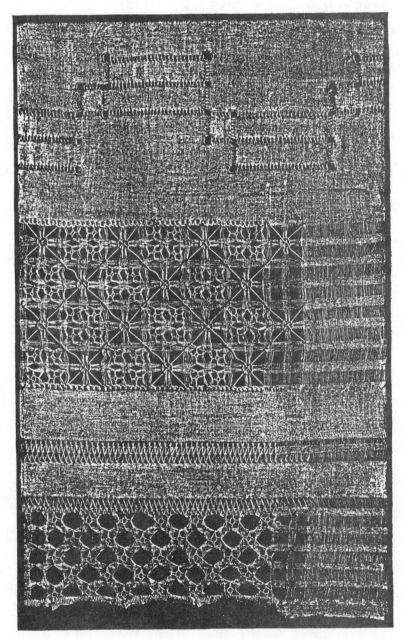

No. 1.—DESIGN FOR A LACE BORDER IN DRAWN-WORK.

DESIGN FOR A LACE BORDER IN DRAWN-WORK.

Among the handsome specimens of drawn-work, those of lace are prominent. They are dainty, easy to make, and adapted to the decoration of many articles and garments for adults and infants.

No. 1.—A very handsome border or finish for an infant's dress or petticoat, or for a lady's apron or

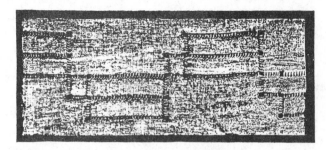

No. 2.

any article she may wish to decorate in this manner is here illustrated. As represented the fabric is very fine but closely woven linen, and the knotting thread is of the usual cotton. If a scarf end of pongee, India-silk or silk bolting cloth were to be decorated by this design, then embroidery silk used for the knotting would produce a very rich and charming result.

DETAILS FOR LACE BORDER.

Nos. 2, 3, 4, 5, 6, 7, 8, 9, 10, 11 AND 12.—In making the lower or lace portion, first turn the edge under like a narrow hem (see No. 4 for width) and

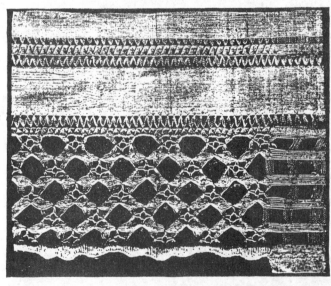

No. 4.

baste it to position, and, after drawing the threads as illustrated, work a scolloped edge in button-hole stitch as seen in the engraving. Secure the edges and strands along the upper edge with the fancy heading represented, first basting *under* the wide

band of fabric between the headings, an extra strip of the material to produce the effect of a hem.

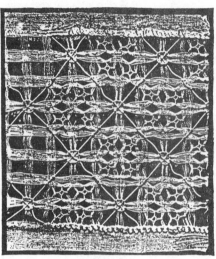

No. 3.

NOS. 2 AND 3.—DETAILS FOR LACE BORDER.

Fasten the upper edge of this strip by the next or second fancy heading.

Now knot the strands and fill in the spaces by the method which is made perfectly plain at Nos. 4 and 5. Or, if preferred, the designs seen at Nos. 6, 7 and 8, or any of the other border designs given elsewhere in this pamphlet may be substituted for the one suggested.

Now draw the threads for the wide band of openwork and secure the edges by the fancy stitching seen at each side

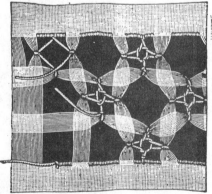

No. 5.

NOS. 4 AND 5.—DETAILS FOR LACE BORDER.

of it. Details for this stitching are given at Nos. 9 and 10. In making the first step of the stitch, set the needle as seen at No. 9, but insert it from the *back* of the edge so that the first step will produce a sort of overcasting along the edge. Next pass the needle up

stitutes the " Deshilado " or genuine Spanish drawn-work. Mexican drawn-work is very similar to Spanish drawn-work, and both are of fairy-like fineness, some of the work looking almost like the

No. 6.

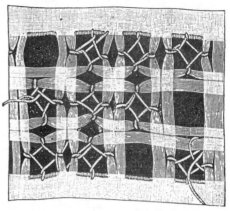

No. 7.

through the last stitch (see No. 10) to finish the knot, and then proceed with the first detail (No. 9) again. Then fill in the spaces and knot the strands as seen in the engravings. No. 11 gives the detail for this band in its full size so that no specific instructions will be necessary, inasmuch as the knotted circles have been previously described in chapter XV. No. 12 shows another variation which may be used in place of No. 11 if desired.

All of the different designs shown at Nos. 6, 7, 8, 11 and 12 are beautiful when executed on very fine fabric. To render such work perfect, but few threads at a time should be drawn each way, and the small sections thus formed gradually filled in. Draw the same number of threads from each direction, say four or five only, and leave the same number of

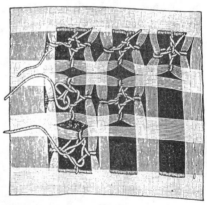

No. 8.

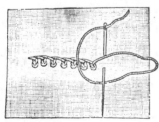

No. 9.

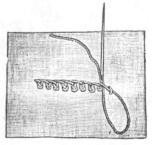

No. 10.

NOS. 6, 7, 8, 9 AND 10.—DETAILS FOR LACE-BORDER.

threads in the intervening spaces. This will make the spaces and squares uniform in size and shape, and converts the fabric into a sort of canvas of exquisite fineness. It is this process that constitutes

dainty webs spun by the deft and cunning spider.

Many of the Spanish and Mexican doilies have entire centers of this exquisite canvas-work, while their borders are composed of dainty hems, fringes or hand-embroidered scollops, or small, obtuse points of the "saw-tooth" style.

The heading seen above the broad open-work band is very easily executed in hemstitching, and to render the work more effective, extra blocks of

No. 11.

the fabric are basted under the little squares and fastened to position by the hemstitching after the method described for introducing block work on page 70. This heading is, like the other band below it, or the lower border, very pretty when used alone or in connection with some other design. The effect of each as separated from the other two, may be seen at Nos. 2, 3 and 4 on page 54.

ANCIENT DRAWN-WORK.

No. 13.—This engraving represents one of the antique specimens of drawn-work referred to on the opening page of this book, and proves that even many decades ago there were women proficient in this most fascinating branch of needle-craft. From the first drawn-work found trace of—away back in the twelfth century —up to the present time, its development has been as marked as that of any other branch of needle-work; and though in the matter of stitches its field has been less extensive than that of embroidery, some of the specimens belonging to the present day, show the most elaborate combinations of its few foundation stitches with the many strands of the fabric-threads, and present effects that are fairy-like in their beauty.

The student in drawn-work will undoubtedly utilize the hint found in this picture of ancient drawn-work and apply its teachings in decorating

some dainty article which she wishes to be of lace-like delicacy. In fact, on other pages of this book will be found illustrations of various articles which are made upon this plan, though, of course, differing in design. At No. 13 it will be seen that many threads were drawn and but few left, and that the spaces thus formed were, individually, of a generous size. This part done, the strands were tightly wound each way and joined at their intersections with fine knotting cotton; and then came the final steps of the work—the filling in of the spaces. This was done with fancy stitches, which, at a later period were adopted by lace-makers, only a few

No. 12.

NOS. 11 AND 12.—DETAILS FOR LACE BORDER.

of whom will admit that lace stitches had their origin in drawn-work. In our book on Modern Lace-Making will be found numerous stitches, all as well adapted to filling in a foundation of net-work formed by drawing some threads of a fabric and leaving others, as to a foundation formed of fancy lace-braids. The filling-in may be uniform throughout the work, or, varying designs, alternately arranged, may be selected.

No. 13.—ANCIENT DRAWN-WORK.

In developing drawn-work of this description, any of the fabrics before mentioned will be found appropriate. Native Eastern fabrics such as *pani* and Broussa silk gauze, both of which are hand-made, would be particularly adaptable. If, however, they cannot be obtained, scrim or silk bolting cloth will prove fair substitutes for them, and form dainty foundations for fine work.

CHAPTER XVIII.

DESIGN FOR DRAWN-WORK LACE, WITH DETAILS.

One of the prettiest results in drawn-work in the form of a pointed lace suitable for the decoration of many kinds of household and personal linen, is here illustrated. The engraving repre-

sents it as considerably less than its actual size, but the details of its design are of full size.

at No. 1. The threads for the top and right side must first be drawn, and measurements exactly made in order to produce regular work.

No. 3 shows the knotting used for the peaks.

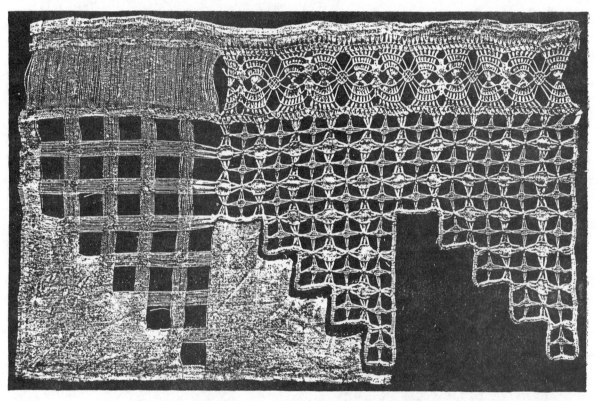

No. 1.—Design for Drawn-Work Lace.

DESIGN FOR DRAWN-WORK LACE, WITH DETAILS.

Nos. 1, 2, 3, 4, 5, 6 and 7.—Two completed points or peaks, and one fully prepared for working are shown at No. 1; while at No. 2 may be seen the regular plan by which the threads are to be cut and drawn, although in this engraving the number and arrangement of the squares slightly differ from the same points in the specimen seen

The basis of the knotting has been given at No. 3, on page 50, where the transforming of the tiny solid squares between the open spaces into circles, is fully illustrated and explained. The remainder of the filling in of this design is illustrated at Nos. 4, 5, 6 and 7 in this chapter, and is conducted as follows: When the circles are knotted, then cross all the squares in one direction—say perpendicularly as seen in the left hand line of spaces at No. 4. Then begin at the right hand of a space (at the middle of its side), fasten the cotton, carry it to the center and here knot it to the intersecting cotton; then carry it across to the opposite side, knot it around the strand and bring it back and knot it at the left of the center knot (see upper left corner of No. 4); then knot it around the *upper* half of the vertical or perpendicular thread, next around the right half of the horizontal thread, and then around the *lower* half of the vertical thread (see engraving just mentioned for all these knottings) and finish the circle by a knot made against the first one. Then carry the cotton under the first knotting at the left, make a knot between the upper two left hand knots and carry the cotton upward and through the knotting of the strand above (see middle square, second row, No. 4) and knot it around both cottons below (see first square, lower row, No. 4); then bring it down and make a knot between the lower two right hand knots (see upper left square, No. 5). This will leave three cottons at the top of the space. Work in the same way to the right of the center and also below it; the cotton will then be at the left hand side of

ing heavy knotting cotton along the edges and then working closely over-and-over it with embroidery

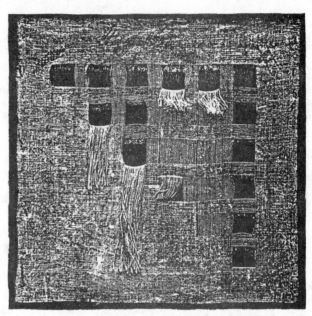

NO. 2.—DETAIL FOR DRAWING THE THREADS.

cotton. Thus finished, it forms a very strong, pretty border or insertion, which may be used above a hem, a fall of fringe or an edging of torchon, Smyrna or modern lace.

Strong darning cotton may also be used under the button-holed edge of the lace to give it a round, firm effect. The button-holing is done when the filling-in is completed, and the final process is cutting it away from the linen—a detail that

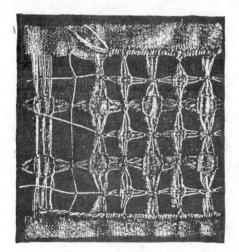

No. 3.

the square (see lower left square, No. 5) and can be carried to the knotting of the strand, passed through it and finally knotted as seen in the adjoining square. Or, to make the work more elaborate, the finishing of the knotting just described may be rendered more ornate by making another row of knots before finishing, after the plan seen at No. 6, after which the square may be completed as described and illustrated.

If preferred, the little solid blocks of material may be left unknotted as seen in details Nos. 4, 5 and 6. In detail No. 3, it will be observed that the design is in border form and that a heavy cord finish is made at each side. This is done by bast-

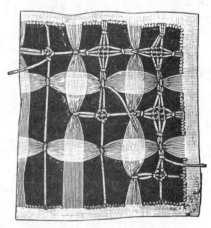

No. 4.

NOS. 3 AND 4.—DESIGN FOR DRAWN-WORK LACE.

must be carefully done in order not to cut the purled edge formed by the stitches.

The heading to this beautiful lace is most easily

made, as may be seen by a close inspection of the completed specimen and detail No. 7. The darned portions may be varied in a number of ways, suggestions for which may be found in different

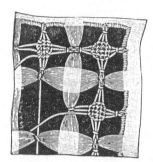

No. 5. No. 6.

designs in this book or may result from personal ingenuity. In knotting the fans, the greater the number of threads used the better will be the foundation for the darned portions, which may be made to assume the shape of leaves, wheels and fancy crosses and figures.

The dainty heading at each side of the main

No. 8.—Ancient Drawn-Work Lace.

heading is too familiar to require a definite description. The eye, aided by the engraving will be a sufficient guide for the fingers.

ANCIENT DRAWN-WORK LACE.

No. 8.—The specimen of drawn-work represented by this engraving has been mentioned and partly described upon page 7 of this pamphlet. It is not only of historical interest, showing as it does that even two centuries ago there were those adequately expert with the needle and possessed of sufficient knowledge of the principles of drawn-work to produce exquisitely delicate results, but it will also afford many suggestions to the needle-woman of the present for creating designs different from any she has ever seen.

It will be observed from the various

No. 7.

Nos. 5, 6 and 7.—Design for Drawn-Work Lace.

unfinished details of the fragment illustrated, that the method we have suggested of drawing but few threads at a time when the design is elaborate, was here adopted. It will further be seen that the tiny figures were traced with fine thread upon the fabric before the threads of the latter were drawn, and that the tracery was over-wrought with some fancy stitch so that in drawing the threads those crossing from selvedge to selvedge could be clipped *outside* of the figure and yet firmly left within it, in order that the figures might appear like appliqué or transferred work when the lace was done.

It will be perceived, also, that the strands are wound and knotted together in a manner which results in a foundation somewhat resembling bobinet. The principle of the knotting is the same as that given in chapter VI., but of course the fabric here represented is of a delicately fine texture and but few strands at a time are wound and knotted, so that the meshes are almost as dainty as those of ordinary net and could be darned in the same manner.

CHAPTER XIX.

DESIGN FOR A HANDKERCHIEF OR TABLE SQUARE, WITH DETAILS.

The engravings illustrating this chapter represent an elaborately decorated square, with details for its construction.   The design and its headings may be used in the ornamentation of handkerchiefs,

![No. 1.—Design for a Handkerchief or Table Square.]

No. 1.—DESIGN FOR A HANDKERCHIEF OR TABLE SQUARE.

from a short distance below the open corner and about an eighth of an inch from the drawn threads *downward* to a point opposite the outer corner (or pencil mark) of the central square ; and is also then cut straight across to this corner. The cutting must of course be done *before the border threads are drawn*, and the cut edges must immediately be button-holed to keep them from ravelling.

Each corner must be cut and button-holed upon the same plan, *but the cut edges will all extend in different directions,* as will be seen by looking at the engraving, and this peculiarity is necessary in order to draw the threads with the result pictured, so that *each side* will *include one corner* in its construction ; this preserves a regularity of the design.   Looking at the corner marked "b" it will be seen that the first cut was made from *left* to *right across* the handkerchief and *then* downward ; whereas in the corner marked "a," as mentioned, the *first* cut was *downward* and the *second* one *across* from *right* to *left.*

In the lower right corner the first cut was *across* from *right* to *left,* and the second *upward* ; while in the remaining corner the first cut was *upward* and the second *across* from *left* to *right.*

The few strands over which the button-hole stitches are made from the sides to

table squares, doilies, tidies, scarfs, etc., etc., but the instructions here given are. for its application to a handkerchief or table square only.

NOS. 1, 2, 3, 4, 5 AND 6.—Having decided upon the material and size desired, cut out the handkerchief and hem it according to the instructions which will be found in chapter XXII., drawing several threads for the hemstitching.   Next draw the second set of threads all around the square, inside of the hemstitching, cutting the fabric at the corners and button-holing the tiny squares along the cut edges as seen in the engraving at No. 1.

Now, having decided according to personal taste and the size of the square how wide you wish the border, prepare for drawing the threads for it as follows : (it will be a good plan to mark off with a pencil the border at each side of the handkerchief, as an extra precaution against making the central square uneven.)   Closely observe the corner marked "a" at No. 1.   You will see that the fabric is *cut*

the central square, must be the same ones which form the first outer band of fabric around the square and also pass through the button-hole stitches around the larger open corners of this central

No. 2.—DETAIL FOR DESIGN

square, (see engraving), in order to provide a firm foundation for the knotting threads used to form and connect the work.

When all the corners are button-holed then the threads for the border and those of the central square may be drawn as seen in the picture, after which the headings may be made just inside of the hem and around the central square. Either or two of the three headings pictured at Nos. 4, 5 and 6 may be used, but the one selected in this particular instance is the one seen at No. 4.

When these headings have been completed you will find your border knotted into strands ready for the design; and then the square must be put into the frame in order to keep the work even as it progresses.

Nos. 2 and 3 fully illustrate the plan and detail of the knotting, and it will be seen by closely inspecting them and the border at No. 3, that the number of strands employed for a fan may vary with personal taste, *six*

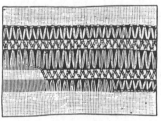

No. 8.

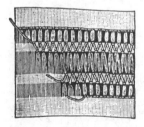

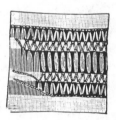

No. 5.   No. 6.

Nos. 3, 4, 5 and 6.—Details for Design for a Handkerchief or Table Square.

seen in No. 2, then another set, (both at the top and bottom of the design) is knotted *back and forth* across the *unworked* fans from the adjoining sides of every pair of *open spaces*, until the alternate fans are knotted to correspond with the knotted ones seen at No. 3, and all the first sets of knotting threads are crossed and knotted to correspond with the diamond-shaped knotted spaces seen at No. 2. The full intention of the knotting design is plainly seen in the finished portion of the border at No. 1. When the knotting is completed, then the edges of the open diamonds are neatly button-holed and may be left as seen in the pictures or filled in with spiders, rosettes, crosses or any fanciful design desired. The corners may also be filled in in the same way. Many times lace stitches are used in forming a net-work in these openings

being selected in the border, and but *four* in the details which describe the knitting.

When the first two sets of cottons have been knotted to form the open and filled-in diamond as

without regard to any special figure or design.

Pongee or India silk scarfs or squares decorated by this design, will be found very charming accessories to the adornment of a home.

CHAPTER XX.

Design for a corner in drawn-work, with method of making.

The formation of a corner in an elaborate design in drawn-work involves considerable work; but if the maker sets about it in the right way she will find the task considerably simplified. The instruc-

Before describing the design it will be well to explain the method of making the fringe, as preparations for the latter form the preliminaries to the drawing of the rest of the threads.

No. 1.—Design for a Corner in Drawn-Work.

tions found in this chapter will be of great service to her in work of this class.

DESIGN FOR A CORNER IN DRAWN-WORK, WITH METHOD OF MAKING.

No. 1.—A very handsome corner for a tray or carver's cloth, a table square, tidy, or any article to have a corner decoration, is here illustrated.

The fringe is double, as a result of first widely hemming the square. Having decided how deep you wish the fringe to be, fold the hem to that depth, draw a few threads as is usual in drawn-work hems, and fasten the hem by the customary hemstitch. This done, draw two or three threads from the *upper side* of the hem an eighth of an inch below the hemstitching, and with the fell stitch used in ordinary hemming fasten the *upper* and *under* sides of the hem together along the drawn space, so that when the fringe is ravelled out (up to this space), the two sides of the hem will not separate and spread the fringe apart.

Although the fringe is not ravelled until the rest of the work is completed, it will be best to mention the method now in order to avoid referring to it again. When ready to finish the fringe, *cut the hem open along the fold,* and ravel its threads in the usual manner. At each corner a square space will occur, and this, if desired, may be filled in as seen in the engraving, by a small piece of doubled fringe, prepared purposely and therefore to match the fringe on the square; but it must be so carefully attached that the joining will be hardly perceptible. The little space that will occur from turning the corner of this additional fringe may be filled in with lace stitches.

NO. 2.—METHOD OF FORMING CORNER, AND DETAILS FOR BORDERS.

After the hem is made as just described, then draw the threads for the three rows of borderings, and separate the strands by the fancy hemstitch represented. The threads are drawn from side to side in the usual manner, thus leaving open spaces at the corners which are afterward filled in with the wheels, darned work and lace stitches, as seen in the picture.

METHOD OF FORMING CORNER, AND DETAILS FOR BORDERS.

No. 2.—This engraving shows the details for two methods of completing a corner, one of which represents the one used for the large corner of No. 1, while the other is that seen in the small corners. It further illustrates the details for the borders.

The right side corner is the first one mentioned. It will be seen that one strand is left beyond the knotted strands at each end of the border, and these are used for the foundations of the extra threads that have to be added to provide for the darning. The extra threads cross the center at right angles, and are knotted to the single strands

mentioned just where they would come if carried across from the fans. The cut edges of the corners should be neatly over-handed before the crossing threads are attached.

The knotting threads of the fans provide sixteen crossing-threads; but as there are sixteen spokes in the corner and each spoke is darned over *three* threads, forty-eight radiating threads will be needed; therefore eight additional crossing-threads will be required, three being added at each side of the space, and one from each corner. (See No. 2).

When these threads have all been arranged, then the single strands at the sides are closely button-holed after the manner seen at No. 1; and this done the darning is begun and carried out as illustrated, or it may be varied to suit the individual taste of the worker. The remaining corner of No. 2 shows how the knotting threads of the fans cross the corner space to form the foundation for the wheels. Two additional threads should cross from corner to corner; and then when all the threads are grouped at the center by a knot, proceed to darn the wheel or any other fanciful figure desired. The knotting of

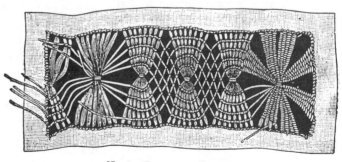

NO. 3.—DETAIL FOR BORDER.

the fans as here illustrated, is done with *three* cottons instead of *two,* as seen at No. 1; but the principle is the same in both, and is fully explained in chapter XIII., except that in the design in that chapter the crossing cottons are knotted to form a lattice-work effect. In these two variations of the design the cottons are simply knotted together at the center of each diamond-shaped space—a me-

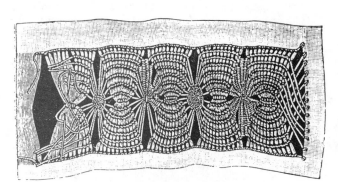

NO. 4.—DETAIL FOR BORDER.

thod which produces a very pretty, lace-like result.

DETAILS FOR THE BORDER.

NOS. 3, 4 AND 5.—No. 3 shows the full detail for the wide border, and fully illustrates how every fourth fan is simply knotted at the center, and its strands, with the knotting cottons from the other fans, are darned into an octagonal star.

No. 4 illustrates another design for such a border, and includes full details for carrying out the work. A greater number of knotting cottons are used, and after they cross the diamond shaped spaces, they are knotted at the center by another cotton which is used in darning the wheels and fancy stars seen in the picture. The fans are separated by winding the cotton about the component groups of strands at the center of each fan, and then a row of knotting is made over this winding by the method which is indicated by the position of the needle and cotton as seen at the last or left-hand fan in the picture.

The wheels are darned in the usual manner over and under the spokes. Each star is begun the same as a wheel, by a knot which draws the crossing threads together at the center. The first or right-hand star has four divisions, each division being darned over four threads;

and the darning of each division begins at the center knot.

In the second and unfinished star the darning is made in wheel form until the points marked by the small crosses are reached, and then each division is darned separately as before. The object of the wheel-center is to keep the divisions of the star from drawing apart. The size of the wheel may be decided by personal taste if the dimensions herein designated are not in keeping with the ideas of the worker.

No. 5 shows another variation for the border which is exceedingly pretty and may be easily worked from the engraving. In grouping the strands into fans, ten strands are knotted for each open fan, and eight should be tied for each alternating one, the knotting threads crossing the strands as seen at the left side of the engraving. The darning thread is carried over and under the middle six strands, and then over the remaining strands and the knotting threads as seen in the picture. A Maltese-cross effect may be produced by darning all the strands of the fans

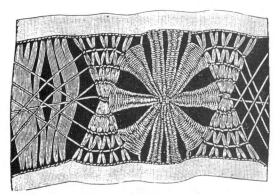

NO. 5.—DETAIL FOR BORDER.

above and below the center, together, and all the cottons together. Very pretty designs for darning crosses and stars may be seen throughout this book.

CHAPTER XXI.

TRAY CLOTH OF LINEN, DRAWN-WORK AND SMYRNA LACE.

The tray cloth here illustrated is made of fine household linen and is decorated with a border and corners of drawn-work, and a frill of fine torchon lace. A variety of patterns are introduced in the border, no two sides and no two corners being alike. The designs for the work were taken from those previously given, and also

detail given at No. 6, and the headings by No. 8 in chapter III.

The upper border is made by the detail given at No. 3 in chapter X, and its headings are formed by detail No. 7 in chapter IV.

The *lower* left corner represents detail No. 7; the *upper* left corner, detail No. 3; the upper right

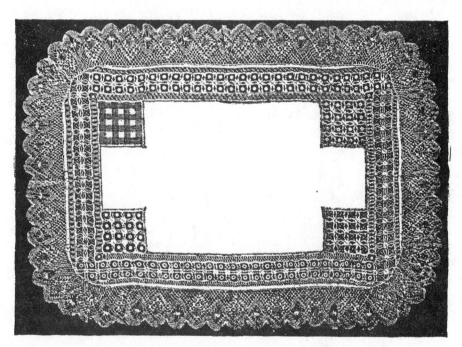

No. 1.—Tray Cloth of Linen, Drawn-Work and Smyrna Lace.

include those immediately following the illustration of the tray cloth.

TRAY CLOTH OF LINEN, DRAWN–WORK AND SMYRNA LACE.

No. 1.—The main portion of the border seen at the *right* side of the tray cloth, is made like the design or detail seen at No. 5, while the heading at each side of it is like that seen at engraving No. 3 in chapter IV.

The border at the *left* side represents the detail disclosed at No. 4, while the headings are made like No. 9, in chapter III.

The border at the lower edge is made after the

corner, detail No. 8; and the remaining corner detail No. 6 in chapter IX.

The little finish generally added to all headings and fully illustrated at detail No. 3 in chapter III., is also adapted to and used for the inner edges of each corner-section, as may be seen by a close inspection of the engraving.

The outer corners of the cloth are not rounded off until the drawn-work is completed, and then the lace frill is added. This frill may also be made of drawn-work by the designs seen in chapters XVII. and XVIII., but the lace here seen renders the article far more dainty in effect.

The cloth may also be enlarged, while making it, by the introduction of a row of insertion matching the lace, before the latter is added.

DETAILS FOR FORMING THE CORNERS.

No. 2.—Having fully described the cloth, we will now give the primary instructions for making it. These consist of a description of the preprations for drawing the threads and shaping the corners as seen at No. 2.

When you have cut out the cloth as large as you desire it to be, decide how wide you want the hem (the one in the cloth illustrated is about one-eighth of an inch wide), and then fold and baste it firmly in place. Next mark off the corners with a sharp pencil, and button-hole stitch each as seen in the picture. Then draw the threads for the hemstitching,

NO. 2.—DETAILS FOR FORMING THE CORNERS.

worked, then draw them for each of the corners.

After the the threads for the border are drawn, fasten the cloth firmly to the frame and proceed to work after the designs and details previously named; and when the border is done, then work the corners after the designs also mentioned for them.

DETAILS USED FOR THE DRAWN-WORK FOR TRAY CLOTH.

Nos. 3, 4, 5, 6, 7 and 8.—The design seen at No. 3 needs no description, as its details are fully represented. The point most especially sought in making this design is an even-meshed net-work in which appear the tiny solid undrawn squares of the fabric. To obtain this result, the knot chain is used in separating the strands, and care is taken to have each of the latter, in bulk, as nearly as possible the size of the knotting thread or cord. The worker must also be very careful to divide her strands and carry her knotting threads so that the tiny squares will be uniform in size and as nearly regular in shape as possible. This will be somewhat tiresome, but not difficult to do.

Nos. 4 and 5 are nearly alike in effect. In previous designs the method and detail of similar knotting has been fully ex-

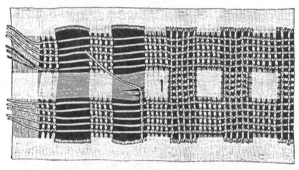

No. 3.

and make the hem as pictured.

To fully explain the theory of making the hem, the hemming has been illustrated as being carried beyond the curve, but in making it the threads should only be drawn to the curve and cut off a short distance from it, in order that the button-hole stitches may firmly secure the corners where they cross the ends of the hemstitching. And when the corners are cut away, great care must be exercised so that the button-hole stitches will not be clipped and thus fray out.

When the cloth is hemmed and the corners are thus far prepared, then draw the threads for the border, and after that is

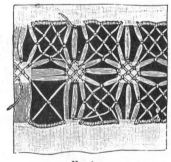

No. 4.

No. 5.

NOS. 3, 4 AND 5.—DETAILS USED FOR THE DRAWN-WORK FOR TRAY CLOTH.

plained, and the engravings here given render further instructions quite unnecessary, as the course of the knotting thread is clearly indicated and may be followed without difficulty.

No. 6 shows a pretty variation in the way of filling in open squares. The knotting is very similar

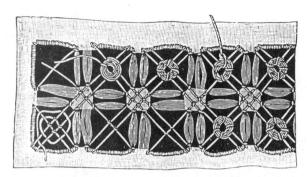

No. 6.—Detail Used for the Drawn-Work for Tray Cloth.

to that given at No. 8 in chapter XI., the chief difference being in the wheels darned about the threads crossing the open spaces. This darning is made with the fourth crossing thread just after the last knot has been made, as will be seen by closely inspecting the thread illustrated in the lower left-hand corner of the engraving. The darning is made around over and under the threads, until as deep as desired, and then a loop is made around the darning between every two sets of threads, the last loop being made so that the thread can then be carried along to finish the knotting crossing the little solid squares.. The second upper square at the right side shows all but the last loop made; this last loop would of course be made in the vacant section and the thread would then be carried along parallel with and like the knotting next to it. In the fourth square a loop has been made to show how to carry the thread along after a final knot. If the fabric is heavy and the knotting cotton light, it is well to make three of these loops in every section instead of one.

No. 7 is very like previous designs. The diagonal crossings are first made, and then one thread is used to make the vertical and horizontal lines and the wheels, and to do the knotting of the strands with. The second knotting of the strands in the upper row shows how to proceed for the first two steps; and the first knotting in the lower row shows the third step; the fourth step would be the dividing of the middle strand and knotting it to the left-side strand. After this the thread would be carried to the center crossings, the wheel darned and a loop to fasten it made at the left side, after which the next knotting of the strands would be begun. (See second wheel, upper row).

No. 8 shows a very lace-like design, and one involving some of the principles of the detail just described. The diagonal crossings are first made, and each tiny solid square is divided into four sections as illustrated, by the looped stitch which is described at Nos. 17 and 18 in chapter XXII. Then a second thread is used to form the vertical and horizontal lines, the long loops and the wheels. The thread (see last space, upper row) is fastened about half of the horizontal strands just under it, then carried to the top of the space, then down and under the vertical and diagonal threads *below* the knot to the vertical strands at the *left;* then back over the diagonal strands and under the loop *above* the knot to the vertical strands at the *right* (see second space, lower row), then back to

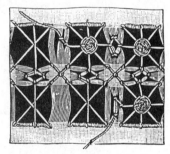

No. 7.

No. 8.

Nos. 7 and 8.—Details Used for the Drawn-Work for Tray Cloth.

the knot where you darn over-and-under to form the wheel. Make a loop-knot when the wheel is completed, and then carry the thread to the point of starting. Work all the square spaces in this manner.

CHAPTER XXII.

DRAWN-WORK DESIGNS FOR HANDKERCHIEFS, DOILIES, SCARFS, TRAY CLOTHS AND VARIOUS ARTICLES OF PERSONAL AND HOUSEHOLD LINEN.

There are many articles of personal and household linen that may be decorated with drawn-work. Among them are those mentioned above as well as shoe-bags of crash and furniture coverings of the same material, which may be decorated with lines of drawn-work intermingled with fancy stitches in

NO 1.—CORNERS FOR A HANDKERCHIEF.

well as towels, buffet scarfs, tidies or any of the numerous little conveniences of the house, such as dust-cloth bags of canvas, laundry bags of linen, colored crewels and worsteds, or any of the colored knotting cottons used for decorative purposes.

Handkerchiefs are particularly pretty when ornamented with drawn-work, and a lady may make such an article for herself from hem to finish, or buy a handkerchief already hemmed and then add the drawn-work.

Doilies decorated with drawn-work for bureau

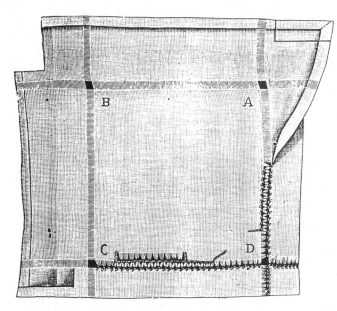

No. 2.—Details for Properly Hemming a Handkerchief.

or toilet cushions are very dainty additions to the appointments of a lady's bedroom or boudoir. They may be made square or oblong and of fine India linen lawn, China silk, pongee or scrim, and may be pure or cream white. Sometimes a little color is introduced by the use of colored knotting thread or of colored silk for the fancy stitches; but as a rule plain white is considered daintier.

Then there are doylies for finger-bowls, cake-baskets and general table use, which may be made of white linen or mummy cloth, in either plain or fancy weaves, and decorated with fringed edges and delicate inner borders of drawn-work, which the tasteful and ingenious woman may fashion with her own skillful fingers. With the designs previously given, together with those immediately following in this chapter, there is no reason why the clever woman with a taste for fancy-work should not make her home belongings as ornate and dainty as heart and eye can desire; nor can she complain that the preceding designs are not suited to any decorative purpose for which she may wish to use them, since they can be applied to articles of personal wear as well as to the development of the "house beautiful."

CORNERS FOR A HANDKERCHIEF.

No. 1.—Just how to make a handkerchief from

the hem to the border and corners will doubt-less prove of interest to those of our readers who, for various reasons, prefer to make these dainty articles for themselves. The fine hand-kerchiefs sold in the shops are expensive and for that reason are beyond the reach of many women who possess a natural desire for tasteful and artistic belongings. Drawn-work handkerchiefs hold a prominent place among the more costly varieties; but she who has carefully followed the preceding lessons can make for herself, with a small expenditure for material, handsome and artistic handkerchiefs.

The handkerchief whose corners are il-lustrated at No. 1 is decorated with a bor-der made after the design in chapter XIII. As the pattern was then fully pic-tured, and as no two corners of the hand-kerchief are alike, we now give very little of the border effect, that the corners may be more perfectly displayed. Two diag-onally opposite corners are decorated with the designs seen respectively in chapters IX. and X., where full instructions for the knotting are given with appropriate illus-trations. In preparing these corners the most careful attention must be given to drawing the threads and to button-holing the cut edges between the threads re-maining after each corner is prepared for knotting. The other two corners are fin-ished with hemstitched effects, one of which may be copied without particular instructions, while the other is explained by the aid of an extra engraving.

It will be necessary to plan out the whole hand-kerchief before beginning to draw the threads, as the border should finish uniformly at each end of all its sides. A reference to the four corners will

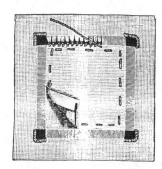

No. 3.—Detail for the Block Corner.

explain exactly what is meant, as just enough of the border is given in each instance to show how and where it ends. In very fine material it will be almost impossible to count the threads, for which reason measurements will have to be substituted.

Having definitely decided upon the spaces and limits, cut the square from the selected fabric, and proceed according to the directions given below.

DETAILS FOR PROPERLY HEMMING A HANDKERCHIEF.

No. 2.—This detail, as here represented, does not belong particularly to the handkerchief under discussion, but applies to the hemming of handkerchiefs in general. When the handkerchief is cut out, draw a thread from each of its four sides to mark the middle of the hem. Then turn under the raw edges in the usual way, and fold the hem down at the drawn thread, in order to find the proper point for the hemstitching that is to be made; and when this point is found, draw as many threads as desired from each side. Then, if the handkerchief is like the one here illustrated, draw the threads that locate the hemstitching around each corner design, button-holing the two raw edges of the tiny square made by cutting out the threads, as seen in the engraving of each corner; and in folding the hems be sure to have the drawn spaces directly over or under each other so that the threads may be taken up evenly and together. This can be accomplished by holding the work up to the light and looking through it when arranging it. But before the hem is basted down ready for hem-stitching, strips should be cut from the corners to reduce the thickness of the hem; and if the plan here given is followed, there will be but one row of overhand or "glove" stitching at each side of the handkerchief.

A close observation of the corners shown at No. 2 will explain the manner of their working. It will be seen that a strip has been cut from corner B and that the edges are finely overcast. At corner C the strip is cut out in an *opposite direction* from that at corner B. The strip to be cut from corner A should correspond in direction with that cut from corner C; and that from corner D must match that at corner B. To put it simply, the direction of the strips taken from the diagonally opposite corners should correspond, in order to make the finish of the hem uniform. In doing the hemstitching, use a much finer thread than that employed for the border and corners, and be careful to secure it very firmly at the corners lest it

become loose in laundering or ordinary wear.

This engraving also shows two or three methods of fancy hemstitching, which may be used upon any handkerchief; but with the elaborate handkerchief, the corners of which are shown in this article, the ordinary hemstitch is most effective.

In the handkerchief illustrated, after the hems have been made, the spaces for the border (one side at a time) are drawn and knotted according to to the instructions referred to in chapter XIII. The corners should be completed last; and as they are represented in full size, no difficulty should be experienced in reproducing them accurately.

DETAIL FOR THE BLOCK CORNER.

No. 3.—This figure very fully represents the method of completing the block corner. The threads are first drawn to form the square in the corner of the handkerchief; then a square of the fabric is cut and narrowly turned under at its edges so that it will exactly fit the *undrawn* square, to which it is basted as illustrated, and then fastened to position by the usual hemstitching process. The raw edges of the tiny corner spaces are neatly button-holed, just as all the raw edges of the various spaces made by cutting out threads are finished.

The present design for a handkerchief is susceptible to many variations. For instance: the corners may all be made alike after one of their patterns, or two designs only may be used instead of four; or, the line of hemstitching marking off the corners may be omitted from the open corners, and the little bands between the borders and corners may be left plain or decorated with feather stitching or any other fancy stitch desired. It will be seen that these methods of completing handkerchief corners may be applied with other border designs and to any article which is to be decorated on all of its sides; and the ingenious needlewoman will be quick in applying the substance of what she has already learned to the development of innumerable corner designs for the many pretty borders hitherto given.

The handkerchief is very handsome made of India silk or pongee The designs illustrated may also be applied to any article of personal or household linen for which they may be suitable.

A WORD OR TWO OF ADMONITION.

Although the student in Drawn-Work has, from time to time, been cautioned to do her work carefully and be precise in its preparation, it will not be a waste of time or words to admonish her still further.

In drawing threads be sure to cut them at exactly the right point so that they will not extend beyond, or fall short of the desired line and thus produce an untidy, unfinished appearance.

Make the knotting as exact as possible as to space and size, and in beginning a piece of work or removing a knotting thread, conceal the beginning or joining, as the case may be, in a neat and strong manner.

In basting work into a square frame or arranging it over a hoop, see that the threads of the warp and filling cross at right angles, as they should when not pulled out of line as they often are by a careless adjustment of the work.

Keep your needle dry and bright with the emery bag; and if the fingers become moist from perspiration, rub the hands in starch or toilet powder; for dry hands are necessary to successful results.

DOILY FOR A PIN CUSHION.

No. 4.—A very dainty little affair made of the finest linen lawn and embroidery silk is here illlustrated. The actual size of the doily from which the picture was made is about five and one-half inches square, but it may be made as large or as small as desired. In making it first cut out the doily as large as you wish it to be, fringe and all. Then at a line where the fringe is to begin at each side, draw two or three threads. Then pass over a space of about an-eighth of an inch, and draw threads for a space of the same width. Next knot

Now draw or ravel the threads for the fringe, wrapping silk around strands at the corners, as seen in the engraving, in order to draw the threads into each opening and thus prettily and strongly complete the corners.

Any tint preferred to the blue may be used in making this doily; and, if preferred, Dresden embroidery may be used for the blossoms—that is, dainty sprigs done in the natural tints and shadings of the flower and foliage may be embroidered upon the lawn. In this event, white silk or any tint used in the embroidery may be selected in finishing the edge of the doily and knotting its fringe.

No. 4.—Doily for a Pin Cushion.

the strands back and forth over the undrawn space as seen in the engraving (and by the familiar heading method), using first white silk, and then going over the same knotting a second time with blue silk. Then add the brier stitching with blue silk, using the latter also, and white, to embroider the blossoms, as seen in the engraving. When the fancy stitching and the embroidery are done, mark out the square in the opposite corner, draw the threads, and knot the strands with blue silk, making a dot of the latter at the center of each little solid square of the fabric.

By the exercise of a little care, the embroidery may be made alike on both sides.

Silk bolting cloth is pretty for such doilies, and any silk gauze-like fabric that is not too delicate, will be found very dainty indeed for articles of this description. The Eastern fabrics mentioned elsewhere in this book, if they can be obtained, would make beautiful doilies of this description; but as any very transparent material whose threads may be drawn will result quite as satisfactorily, the maker of a doily may feel perfectly satisfied in using any sheer domestic or imported fabric.

INFANTS' SHIRTS, DECORATED WITH DRAWN-WORK.

NOS. 5, 6, 7 AND 8.—The dainty little garments illustrated at Nos. 5 and 7 and 8, are both planned and made upon the same principles as regards the for the back and one for each side of the front, and each front edge is a selvedge of the fabric.

A most important item is the cutting out of the

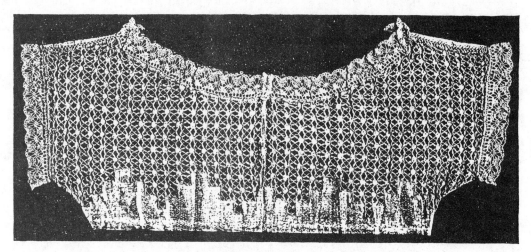

No. 5.—INFANTS' SHIRT, DECORATED WITH DRAWN-WORK.

application of the design and the preparation of the fabric for the work. The same plan also applies to yokes of gowns, chemises, dresses and aprons, and also for articles having rounded or irregular corners. The garments are both made of fine, close linen, and are finished with torchon lace. No. 5 is in three sections—one for the back and two for the front. The other, seen at Nos. 7 and 8, is in one piece only and has under-arm seams made in the usual way; but the same plan as the one given below for No. 5 should be incorporated in the preparations for making it. The design used in the points and the little fancy squares on the shoulders will be found in chapter IX. For the garment illustrated at No. 5, detail No. 4 in chapter XV. was selected for the ornamentation, which is applied in yoke style at the front only. As before mentioned, the garment is in three sections—one

garment, which should be done as follows : Having obtained or made your pattern of the size described, lay each portion to be decorated upon a square-cornered section of the linen, and with a pencil mark the outline of the garment, but *do not cut the outlined portions out until the drawn-work is completed.* Next draw the threads as suggested by No. 6, *always keeping within the outlined portions.*

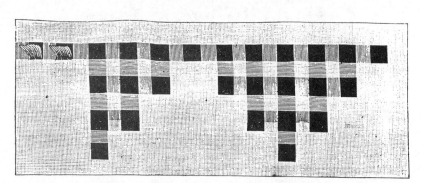

No. 6.—METHOD OF DRAWING THE THREADS.

Next fasten each front section, as worked, in a frame (which could not be conveniently done if the garment were cut out at the outlines), and then fill in the drawn-work as seen at No. 5. Then remove the work from the frame, cut the garment

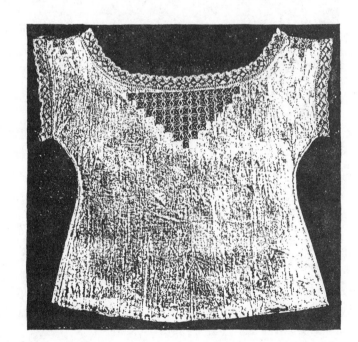

No. 7.—INFANT'S SHIRT, DECORATED WITH DRAWN-WORK. (FRONT VIEW.)

and handsome designs that may be adopted after the method just described for decorating these tiny garments of babyhood, or applied to other garments belonging to an infant's *layette*.

There is no daintier finish for the yoke of a little slip, or a robe for day or night wear, than drawn-work, and as it is really a part of the garment so decorated, it possesses the advantage of as perfectly enduring the frequent ordeals of the laundry which an infant's wardrobe must necessarily encounter, as the fabric itself — a recommendation which cannot be attached to many of the decorations used for such garments.

Robes and slips so ornamented, may have their skirt portions elaborated by broad bands of drawn-work matching the yokes and made between clusters of tucks above a deep hem, or above the hem alone; and both hem and tucks may be finished by hemstitching after the methods illustrated and described in the opening chapters

out just far enough outside of the outline to allow for a very tiny hem on every edge, making the same allowance for the back section. Make this hem on every edge except the front edges of the front, and then by a dainty, fancy herring-bone stitch (see top of sleeve, No. 5), unite the top and back sections at the top of the sleeve and under the arms. Finish the edges with fine torchon or Valenciennes lace, which may also be carried down the overlapping front edge, or down both edges, as seen at No. 7. Fine close linen or linen lawn may be used for a little garment of this description.

Dainty yokes may be made of clusters of hand-run fine tucks alternating with strips of drawn-work which should be made in the fabric between the clusters. It is not advisable to make the tucks on a sewing-machine, as such work, unless the tension of the machine is under perfect control, is liable to draw cr pucker and thus disfigure the whole effect. Throughout this pamphlet will be found various

No. 8.—INFANT'S SHIRT, DECORATED WITH DRAWN-WORK. (BACK VIEW.)

of this pamphlet. A pretty variation results from finishing the hems mentioned with fancy stitching.

No 9—Drawn-Work Doily.

DRAWN-WORK DOILY, WITH DETAIL.

Nos. 9 and 10.—This doily is one of a set of four each equally as pretty as the one here illustrated, and no two alike. Each is made of fine linen lawn, and fine knotting cotton and silk floss are used in developing the design.

No. 10 shows just how the design is developed, and how the strands are made to take the place of the knotting-cotton spokes so that each star will have eight sections with two spokes to a section; and in darning over these strands all trace of them is removed, and the work looks like a net-work of knotting and darning alone. After the strands are drawn and cut, a row of button-hole stitches must be made around the edges as indicated. Feather stitch the narrow band of fabric next the fringe and then ravel out the latter.

No. 10.—Detail for Doily.

NO. 11.—CARVER'S OR TRAY CLOTH. (FOLDED.)

as with table-mats. The engraving here given presents one corner of a doily in its full size, and clearly illustrates the design and the method of its knotting. The material is fine, heavy linen, and the hem is secured by the method explained at No. 11. Made of finer, very sheer linen lawn, a doily decorated by this design would be very pretty as a cover to a toilet-cushion or to place the latter upon. In sheer fabrics, tinted silk floss might be used for the knotting; and tiny blossoms, worked in tints, would add to the beauty of the effect.

CARVER'S OR TRAY CLOTH. (FOLDED.)

No. 11.—This cloth is made of fine, heavy linen, and is about three-quarters of a yard square, but may be made oblong, if desired. The wide hem is secured by the knot-chain hemstitch, and the strands are again fastened by the knot chain to produce the result seen above the hem of No. 1, in chapter III. The crosses are formed by a familiar design, as will be observed by inspecting the engravings; but, if preferred, each cross may be made by a different design, previous chapters containing a great variety from which to choose. Squares or peaks may be substituted for the crosses, and details for designs of this description will be found in several of the chapters of this pamphlet.

SECTION OF PLATTER DOILY.

No. 12.—Five platter doilies usually comprise a set, the same

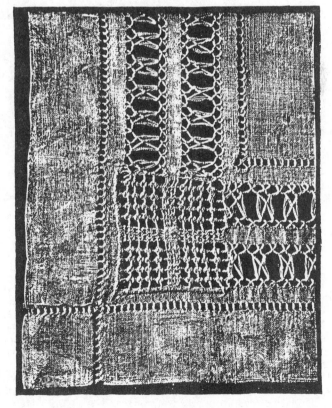

NO. 12.—SECTION OF PLATTER DOILY.

FOUR DESIGNS FOR HANDKERCHIEF CORNERS.

Nos. 13, 14, 15 and 16.—The four corners of a fine linen-lawn handkerchief are here illustrated, and are given in full size. The process of hemming a handkerchief has been previously given and needs no repetition here. This part of the work must be carefully done, and many ladies avoid it altogether by buying a fine handkerchief already hemmed and then adding such designs in drawn-work as please them best.

The details for one corner only are given, as the

a long button-hole stitch as seen in picture No. 17. Then the horizontal set of cottons which twist the vertical strands as illustrated are inserted; and after this the next set of diagonal threads are added to cross the first corresponding set. The final set of cottons twist the remaining strands, and as each is brought to the center of a space it is knotted around the threads once, and is then carried around the threads in a succession of extra circle-knots (see unfinished circles at No. 18) to the

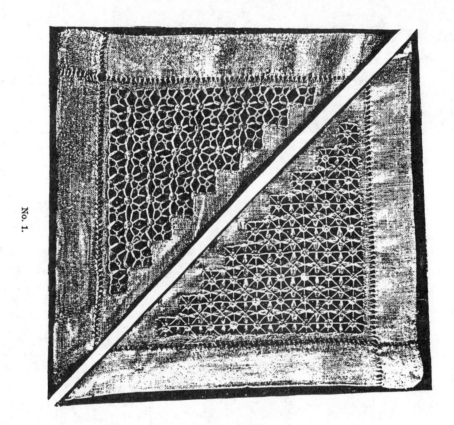

No. 1.

No. 2.

NOS. 13 AND 14.—DESIGNS FOR HANDKERCHIEF CORNERS.

other three corners are duplicates or modifications, of patterns previously given.

DETAILS FOR CORNER No. 3.

Nos. 17 and 18.—These details are for corner No. 3. After the threads are drawn, a tiny hole is made at the center of each solid square of the fabric, and then diagonal cottons are worked in rows and are each fastened into the punctured squares by means of

opposite side, and then passes through the next set of vertical strands to the center of the next space. The result is very pretty; but the method may be varied according to the taste and ingenuity of the worker if the design presented does not quite please her.

In chapter XV. will be found the basis of the design by which the corner represented by No. 1 was decorated; in chapter XVIII. will be found the details for corner No. 4, while corner No. 2 is a modification of the design seen in chapter X.

It is not necessary that the corners differ from each other in the matter of design. They may all

ner, sometimes in alternate corners, and often as a border at each side of a line of drawn-work. The

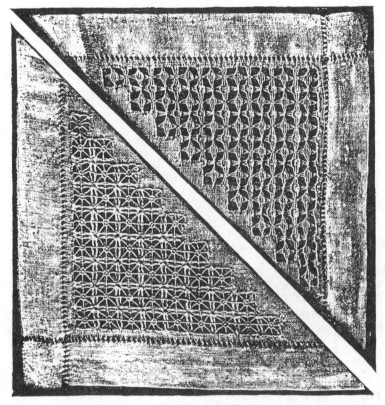

No. 3.

No. 4.

NOS. 15 AND 16.—DESIGNS FOR HANDKERCHIEF CORNERS.

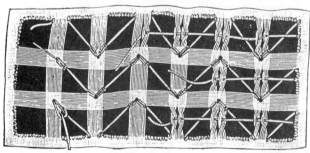

No. 17.

daintiest handkerchiefs are all white ; but tiny dots of color may be embroidered upon the fabric if desired, either in the border or over the center.

Pale-blue and pale-pink handkerchiefs for the corsage are made of silk gauze, and are knotted with silk when they are decorated with drawn-work.

be alike if preferred ; or, the design selected may be used in but one corner or in two. The application of one design, or several, must depend wholly upon the taste of the worker or the lady to whom the handkerchief is to belong when it is completed. Embroidery is often very prettily intermingled with drawn-work in the decoration of a handkerchief, sometimes appearing in each cor-

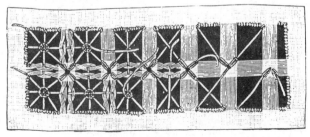

No. 18.

NOS. 17 AND 18.—DETAILS FOR CORNER NO. 3.

DESIGN FOR A DOILY.

Among the daintiest articles decorated with drawn-work are pretty little square or oblong doilies to lay over satin toilet cushions or bureau scarfs after the fashion of mats, upon which may

No. 19.—CORNER OF DOILY.

be placed perfume jugs, powder boxes, Cologne bottles, etc. In many of the doilies white embroidery silk is intermingled with the working cotton in a most effective manner.

Any of the fancy designs illustrated and described in previous chapters may be used in decorating articles of this kind, and the application may include variations for the corners, a handsome and dainty illustration of such an addition being represented at No. 19.

DESIGN FOR DOILY, WITH DETAIL FOR THE CORNER.

Nos. 19 and 20.—These engravings illustrate a doily or scarf for a toilet cushion, the material used being sheer linen lawn. The design is very similar to those which appeared in chapters VII. and VIII., and the border is made upon exactly the same principles as are described for those designs, so that any one who has mastered either

pattern mentioned will have no difficulty in following the one here shown.

In order to render the corner design perfectly clear as to detail, we have added a quarter-section of the circle, with the threads spread out so as to fully illustrate their arrangement, although in chapter VIII. the method of making the solid center of the circle is distinctly shown. Button-hole stitches must be made along the inner edges of the corner as seen at figure No. 19, to stay them before the radiating threads are attached. The knotting thread which forms all the fans and the spokes or radiating threads of the web or circle is cotton; but the solid portion of the circle and the ring about it, as well as the fancy stitching at each side of the border, are made of white embroidery silk. The contrast thus formed is exceedingly pretty.

In making the fringe, which is done last, draw two or three threads at each side of the doily where the fringe is to be knotted; then by means of the knot chain tie the threads into strands as thick as they are desired to be. When the strands are tied, draw or ravel the remainder of the fabric intended for the fringe, and the latter will be complete.

This design may be tastefully used for bureau scarfs, tidies, handkerchiefs, pillow shams or any arti-

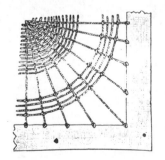

No. 20.—DETAIL FOR THE CORNER.

cle which is to be decorated with a border and corners. Plain hems or lace frills often complete the border.

No. 21.—FANCY DOILY IN DRAWN-WORK.

FANCY DOILY IN DRAWN-WORK.

Nos. 21 AND 22.—This dainty piece of work is easy of accomplishment, as will be seen by referring to figure No. 22, where an enlarged section of the center is given as a detail. After the square spaces made by the strands have been filled in with knotting as seen in the detail, the cotton is wound round and round the strands to produce a cord-like effect, and at their crossings rosettes or spiders are made. At each side of the knottings tiny fan-like sections are formed by the darning process used in making the rosettes. Before the work is begun, or as soon as the strands are drawn, the edges should be buttonholed to keep them from fraying. The doily is represented of full size, and is completed with a row of fancy hemstitching be-

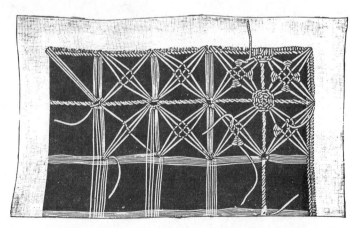

No. 22.—DETAIL FOR FANCY DOILY IN DRAWN-WORK.

tween two strips of the material left from drawing the threads. These strips are ornamented with feather stitching done in wash embroidery silk. The edge is fringed out as seen in the picture after a row of knot chain stitching has been made to confine the strands. The material used is fine linen lawn and the doily may be used for pin cush-

engraving, button-hole stitches being used at all the corners to keep the fabric from fraying out.

When the large corners are button-holed, six threads cross the space to form the foundation for the stars and make the oblique lines seen. The

NO. 23.—TABLE DOILY OF LINEN AND DRAWN-WORK.

ions, finger bowls, punch glasses or for any of the many purposes to which such articles are put.

TABLE DOILY OF LINEN AND DRAWN-WORK.

No. 23.—This doily is about five and one-half inches square, and is made of very fine butcher's linen, and decorated with pale-blue linen floss. The hem is finished in the usual manner, by a hemstitch. Then the threads are drawn for the cross and the strands are wound as seen in the

star-points are darned in, the two central threads at each side, with one of the central threads from the opposite side forming the foundation for every two points. The work of the darning will be more easily comprehended from the picture than by description, as the engraving shows just how and where it is made.

Doilies of this variety may be made of sheer linen or from India silk or pongee, or any fabric from which the threads may be easily drawn and secured. The floss used may be of any tint preferred or of white, either completing a doily prettily.

NO. 24.—FINGER-BOWL DOILY.

The center designs may be procured at any embroidery store; or the clever woman of artistic taste and skill may design them for herself and trace them with ink, or a sharp pencil, or transfer them from tracing paper to the fabric.

CORNER FOR A CARVER'S OR TRAY CLOTH.

No. 25.—This engraving shows the corner of a carver's or tray cloth made of white linen of a firm but light texture. Chapter III. fully explains the border, and chapter X. includes the principles for making the corner. The maker of a cloth like this one must remember that the engraving represents the work only about half size, but the sets referred to give the details in their full size.

FINGER-BOWL DOILY.

No. 24.—The correct size of the doily here illustrated is seven inches square, including the fringe, which is one inch wide. The drawn-work border is three-eighths of an inch wide, and is represented in full size and fully described at No. 8 in chapter XVI., with the exception of the corners. These are of the wheel or spider-web design which has been so frequently described before. Engraving No. 3 in chapter VIII. represents an excellent method for making the wheels or web for this variety of doily. Knotting cotton is alone used for the doily, the fringe of which is made the same as that finishing the doily represented at No. 28. The design at the center of the doily is stamped and may be embroidered in outline stitch with blue or red cotton.

6

NO. 25.—CORNER FOR A CARVER'S OR TRAY CLOTH.

No. 26.—Drawn-Work Doily.

No. 27.—Detail for Corner of Doily.

DRAWN-WORK DOILY, WITH DETAIL FOR CORNER.

Nos. 26 and 27.—This charming doily needs no
special instructions for making it, as the engraving,
which is full size, depicts the design and finish
most perfectly; and the maker will be sufficiently
assisted by the detail of the corner seen at No. 27
to properly complete it. At all of the edges where
the strands are cut away, button-hole stitches must
be made as seen in the engraving, to prevent the
fabric from fraying. The feather stitching is done
with wash embroidery silk, and though here represented as white, may be of pale-blue or pink.
If desired the knotting and darning may be of silk.

DESIGN FOR A BUREAU DOILY.

No. 28.—This exquisite little article is made of fine linen lawn. It is, of course, represented smaller than its proper size, which is six and a-half inches

frame the rest of the threads are ravelled. The fancy stitching may be done while the work is on the frame or after it has been removed, as convenient for the worker.

DETAIL FOR BUREAU DOILY.

No. 29.—This engraving represents a section of the doily full size, except that the knotting cotton is illustrated a trifle larger than that actually used, for the benefit of the student. It will be seen that the cut edges of the corners are protected by button-hole stitches made before the knotting is begun; and that next to the upper right wheel the knotting at the edge of the fabric has been omitted, simply to show that, if desired, the doily may be knotted in that way. It will not, however, be as firm as if fully knotted. The knot chain is used to separate the strands in the manner now perfectly familiar to our students; and a close

No. 28.—Design for a Bureau Doily.

square, including the fringe. The knotting of the strands is all done with very fine cotton, which is crossed and knotted in each of the square spaces to form the foundation or "spokes" for the wheels after the method described in previous designs which include similar circles. The wheels or circles, as well as the fancy stitches along the border and other portions of the fabric, are formed of white embroidery silk; and the combination of the delicate fabric, the lace-like strands and the rich silk is most effective. The work is done over a frame, to which the doily is basted after two or three threads have been drawn each way to provide for the knotting of the fringe, and the spaces have been wholly or partly drawn for the strands and cut for the corners. The fringe is made last. It is knotted into strands at the tiny spaces drawn for it, and after the doily is removed from the

No. 29.—Detail for Bureau Doily.

inspection of the detail will perfectly convey the method by which the strands are separated and again knotted together to produce the lattice effect seen in the two engravings. The principle of this knotting has been incorporated in various preceding designs and requires no further special instructions.

In making the wheels, the silk is first attached at

DOILY FOR A PIN CUSHION OR TOILET BOTTLE.

No. 30.—This dainty doily is made of very sheer linen lawn, and is pretty for either of the purposes mentioned in the title given above. The principles involved in the making of a handkerchief, as explained on previous pages, govern the making of

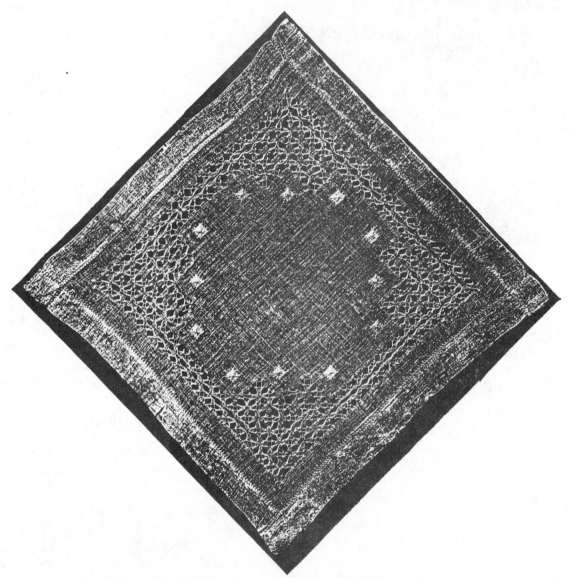

No. 30.—Doily for a Pin Cushion or Toilet Bottle.

the center knotting of the "spokes," and then carried from one to another and wrapped once around each "spoke" with a back-stitch movement. This covers the cotton "spoke" and results in a solid, ribbed, silken wheel. If desired, the wheels and feather stitching may each be made with pale-blue, pink, yellow, green or lavender silk, but the daintiest doilies are those in which no color whatever appears.

the doily, which is, in effect, a miniature handkerchief. Enlarged to the ordinary handkerchief size it would make quite as pretty a handkerchief as, in its present size, it does a doily. As the engraving is perfectly clear and a similar design has been previously given, details will not be necessary. The eye will guide the fingers in carefully developing and applying the design.

DESIGN FOR A HANDKERCHIEF BORDER IN DRAWN-WORK.

No. 31.—At this engraving is shown a hand-

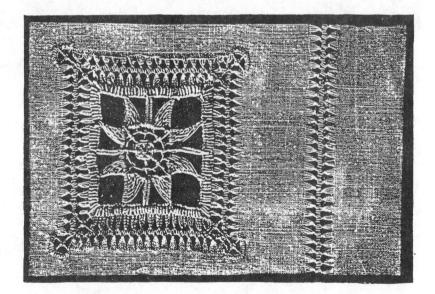

No. 31.—Design for a Handkerchief Border in Drawn-Work.

preferred; but narrow hems, that is, those which are from a-half to one inch wide, are the most popular. If the worker does not wish to hemstitch her handkerchief herself, she may purchase a handkerchief already hemmed and decorate it with the design illustrated or any other she may admire.

DESIGN FOR CENTER AND SIDE OF A BUREAU DOILY.

No. 32.—This doily is nearly six inches square, and the section represented is of full size. It is made from linen with white knotting cotton, the latter being applied as is plainly demonstrated by the engraving. A tiny band of the fabric divides the strands above the hem, and the knotting crosses it twice. A similar band is next the outer edge of the center, and a wider one, over-wrought with button-hole stitches forms the inner edge. Eight threads cross the square space from side to side, and these are darned together and also over-wrought with button-hole stitches to form the star

kerchief decorated after the drawn-work design given in chapter IX. where all the details for its development were clearly described and plainly illustrated. Only a corner section of the handkerchief is here pictured, but the design continues in a border about the entire handkerchief. Frequently this design is used only for a corner, which may be simply a square; or it may extend to the third row of stars at each side and terminate squarely or with an irregular outline similar to that made by stairs or steps. The hem of the handkerchief may be wide or narrow, as

No 32.—Design for Center and Side of a Bureau Doily.

as it is represented in the picture. The center is filled in in spider-web or rosette style.

No. 33.—Doily of Drawn-Work.

DOILY OF DRAWN-WORK, WITH DETAIL FOR THE CENTER.

Nos. 33 AND 34.—In preparing this doily considerable care will have to be taken to preserve the edges of the diamond shaped center from stretching and fraying. Figure No. 34 shows how the work is made from side to side of the diamond along a bias edge instead of back and forth from point to point. The corners are drawn and prepared similarly to the method given for the doily on page 74, except that the cotton crosses the open spaces and solid squares four times instead of twice, so as to provide a sufficient number of threads for darning in the Maltese crosses in the open spaces. The border and fringe are prepared like those of the other doilies previously given, and feather-stitching in silk is added.

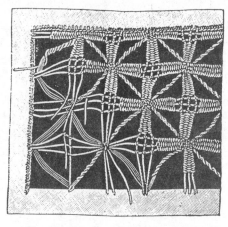

No. 34.—Detail for Center of Doily.

CORNER FOR A DOILY.

No. 35.—This engraving illustrates a corner for a doily or a cover for a pin-cushion. Various portions of designs heretofore illustrated are united in the decoration, and as the engraving pictures them with accuracy, it will be unnecessary to give special details for the work. A row of button-hole stitches is made at each side of the drawn portion before the knotting is begun, in order to prevent the edges from fraying out. The feather-stitching is done with silk, and so are the solid wheels in the spaces and those at the center of the blocks; but the knotting and open wheels are done with thread. In making the solid wheels each spoke is wrapped once around with the silk to produce a ribbed effect. Any of the pretty designs illustrated as borders, or portions of such designs may be used in making these dainty little articles; and, if preferred, only corners need be used, in which event delicate blossoms may be embroidered on the undrawn fabric. The Dresden embroidery, done in silks in natural flower-tints, would be very dainty on such doilies.

Doilies of this description are often used under finger-bowls or punch-glasses, being made much smaller for the latter purpose than for the former. They may be purchased in sets, if a lady does not wish to make them. There may be six

A dainty effect may be obtained in making doilies for cushions, etc., by using colored silk for some of the knottings and wheels, or plac-

No. 36.—CORNER OF CARVER'S CLOTH.

ing the doily over a cushion of a delicate contrasting tint.

CORNER OF CARVER'S CLOTH.

No. 36.—Although termed a carver's cloth, the article, a corner of which is here represented, may also be used for a buffet or tray cloth. It is made of butcher's linen and has a broad hem which is held in place by the drawn-work border with which the cloth is decorated. In size this cloth is about forty-five inches long and twenty inches broad; but it may be made of any dimensions desired and oblong or square, according to the dish it is to be used under. As the method of knotting does not differ in the main from the methods heretofore illustrated, it will not be necessary to explain it in detail. Either the knot chain or the knot hemstitch may be used in separating the strands as preferred, but the latter is desirable on account of the hem the upper edge of which is fastened at the same time the knotting is made. After all the knotting is made the rosettes or "spiders" are made; and instead of weaving over and under the spokes, the thread is carried *around* each as seen in the picture. Very effective drawn-work is made by using unbleached linen floss for the knotting. The soft tint of the linen, with the deeper tone of the floss, results in a most charming combination.

No. 35.—CORNER FOR A DOILY.

or twelve in a set, and no two need be alike. As a rule, all the doilies are different in design.

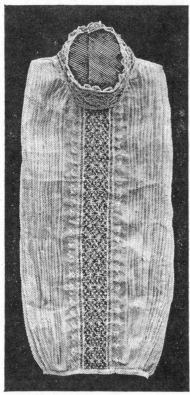

No. 37.—Chemisette of Lawn and
Drawn-Work.

CHEMISETTE OF LAWN AND DRAWN-WORK.

No. 37.—This is one of the daintiest chemisettes imaginable. It is made of fine linen lawn back and front, and has a collar and center-strip of delicate drawn-work underlaid with pink satin ribbon. The top of the collar and each edge of the center-strip are bordered with fine Valenciennes lace; and at each side of the center-strip the lawn is accordion-plaited, tucked and feather-stitched in a most charming manner. The back is shaped like that of an ordinary vest or of any of the fashionable blouse-vests and closes with button-holes.

The picture fails to fully represent the beauty of the chemisette, but will serve to give our readers a new idea for the use of drawn-work. Those who wish to do so may purchase such chemisettes ready made; or, if preferred, they may buy the drawn-work by the strip and make the chemisettes themselves; or, if they have the time, and can make pretty drawn work, they may supply themselves at trifling expense with a number of the dainty garments to be worn with Summer or other coats or jackets. Dressy

coats of velvet or brocaded silk are generally worn over a blouse or chemisette-front, and nothing could be daintier than one combining sheer lawn and delicate drawn-work.

The ribbon chosen to underlie the drawn-work may be of any tint preferred, or, it may be black or white. A pretty effect would be obtained by omitting the ribbon down the center and wearing the chemisette over a closely fitted or blouse front of silk the tint of the collar lining. Yokes could be made of strips of drawn-work alternating with strips of tucked material. This arrangement would be especially pretty for lawn or organdy dresses, whether plain white, tinted or figured.

DRAWN-WORK TOILET CUSHION.

No. 38.—Drawn-work doilies may be put to many uses, and one of the prettiest of them is here illustrated. The doily itself is of the usual elaborate variety used under finger-bowls, trays, toilet bottles, etc., but it is here attractively laid over a round, yellow satin cushion, encircled with three double fluffy ruffles of deep-yellow chiffon. Sometimes four ruffles are used, sometimes two; but no matter whether two or four are used, a toilet cushion of this description is one of the daintiest things seen among the articles for my lady's use. Blue, lavender, pink, Nile-green and various shades of yellow are the

No. 38.—Drawn-Work Toilet Cushion.

tints generally seen in these cushions, which may be purchased for a reasonable sum, or made at home if fingers are deft and skilful.

SLIP FOR INFANTS' PILLOW IN DRAWN-WORK AND LINEN LAWN.

No. 39.—This pretty slip is made of fine linen lawn, drawn-work and Valenciennes lace. The construction is the same as that of an ordinary ornamental pillow-slip, the back being plain and buttoning at one end. The pillow used with a slip like the one illustrated should be covered with pale-pink or pale-blue sateen, Silesia, silk or satin. Hemstitching borders the center, outer edge

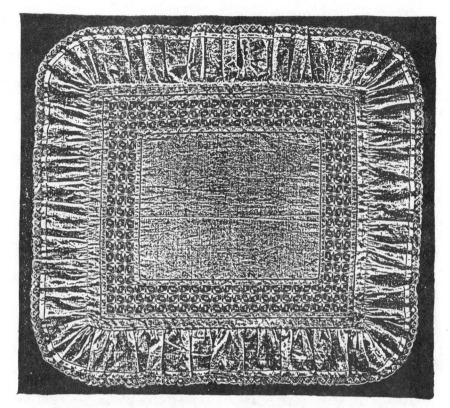

NO. 39—SLIP FOR INFANTS' PILLOW IN DRAWN-WORK AND LINEN LAWN.

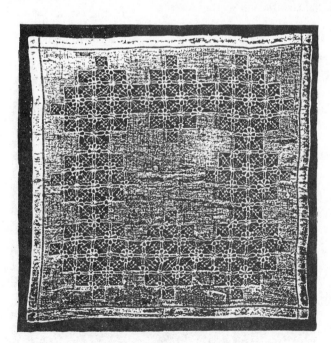

NO. 40.—CENTER-PIECE IN DRAWN-WORK.

slip can be purchased ready-made, or, if a lady prefers, she can buy the materials and put them together herself.

Any number of pretty border designs, with details, are shown in this pamphlet and could be suitably applied in making a slip of this kind.

CENTER-PIECE IN DRAWN-WORK.

No. 40.—This engraving represents one of the prettiest and newest designs for center-pieces, doilies, tray-cloths, etc. It will be observed that the pattern is so arranged that the size of the article to be decorated must always be increased or diminished by one whole block or diamond.

No details of the design can, in this case, be supplied; but on various pages of this pamphlet appear many appropriate and equally pretty designs which may be used in making a similar center-piece.

Directions for hemstitching are also given at the beginning of the pamphlet, and close at hand are designs showing how to cut out material when the pattern is not to extend. from edge to edge of the article.

and ruffle. If preferred, the ruffle might also be decorated with drawn-work. A section of a ruffle of this description may be seen on page 93. The

No. 41.—Corner of Handkerchief in Mexican Drawn-Work.

CORNER OF HANDKERCHIEF IN MEXICAN DRAWN-WORK.

No. 41.—This engraving represents the corner of a handkerchief done in Mexican drawn-work. It is in the new butterfly design, and is an exquisite exponent of this fascinating art. At the present time Mexico is more famed for its drawn-work than any other country, and its products in that line are as dainty as the webs of spiders, as exquisite as the frost on the pane. The design here given may be very easily worked out by any one accustomed to doing fine drawn-work. Fine linen thread should be used in developing the design and hemstitching the borders. The threads for the first row of hemstitching are carefully drawn in the width desired and the hem is then turned up so that the narrow fold at the edge will be even with the lower edge of the drawn space, and the hemstitching is then done by the method illustrated at No. 4, page 12, the lower row catching and holding the hem firmly in place. Any other style of hemstitching may be substituted for the design here given. The inner line of hemstitching is made at the same distance from the border as the outer line. It is best to place the handkerchiefs in an embroidery or drawn-work frame before beginning to knot the strands and darn in the butterflies. The fabric will not then draw up.

FRINGED TUMBLER DOILY.

No. 42.—This exquisite little doily is made of fine linen lawn. As will be observed, it is almost wholly composed of knotting and darning, only a sufficient number of the fabric threads being left to form a foundation for the development of the design. The engraving is full size, and therefore shows the doily as it will appear when finished, except that the transparency of the fabric has been partly lost in the process of reproduction.

No. 42.—Fringed Tumbler Doily.

No. 43.—PIN-CUSHION WITH DRAWN-WORK COVER.

preferred may be used, pink, blue, lavender and green sharing popularity with yellow.

FANCY DRAWN-WORK DOILY.

No. 44.—The doily here shown illustrates the progress recently made in the development of this dainty work from plain, angular designs to those of graceful outlines and delicate curves. The process in the present case is necessarily a careful one and should be undertaken only by an expert. The design must be worked out on a square of linen and the outer edge button-holed before the outer linen is cut away; then a fine picot edge is added. This edge may be made by hand or purchased at a lace-making establishment.

As the doily is one of a number of pretty articles found here and there, we are unable to furnish details of the design; but as in other cases we suggest that the detailed designs given in other parts of the book be applied in making doilies of similar shape.

PIN-CUSHION WITH DRAWN-WORK COVER.

No. 43.—Among the daintiest articles of drawn-work are cushions for ordinary or stick-pins to be placed on the bureau or toilette table. The one illustrated by this engraving is about four inches square and made of muslin covered with yellow satin and then again covered on the upper side with a square of drawn-work. The under side is covered with a square of plain lawn, while a frill of the latter edged with narrow Valenciennes lace borders the two sections and holds them together. Bows of yellow satin ribbon are at the corners. Satin of any other tint

No. 44.—FANCY DRAWN-WORK DOILY.

TABLE-SQUARE IN DRAWN-WORK.

No. 45.—This engraving fully describes to the eye the dainty square it illustrates. The square may be of any size desired according to the dimensions of the table ; or, it may be made but little larger than the engraving, in which event it would serve as a doily.

CORNER IN DRAWN-WORK.

No. 46.—This pattern is for a corner an inch and three-quarters square. Cut out the square and button-hole the edges. Put in threads from corner to corner, using six on each side. Do not carry the last thread put in clear across, but tie all of the threads in a bunch in the center with it. Make the spider by working away from you, putting the needle under each thread, with its point toward you. When the center is large enough, tie the thread around two or three threads of the body where the last half-thread is left out, and tie this thread to the edge where it belongs. Break the thread and tie it around one of the threads half-way between the spider and the end of the thread. Work all around, tying the working thread to each cross thread. Work around the thread again, making a spider on each four threads, weaving them large enough so that their corners will touch.

NO. 45.—TABLE-SQUARE IN DRAWN-WORK.

FANCY DRAWN-WORK DOILY.

No. 47.—Another unique drawn-work doily is here illustrated. It is made of sheer linen lawn and is composed principally of darning and winding, the latter process confining the fabric threads which

NO. 46.—CORNER IN DRAWN-WORK.

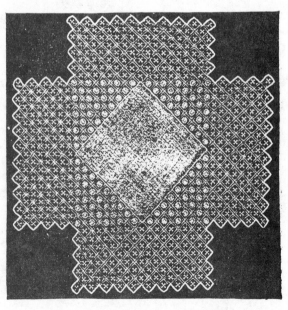

NO. 47.—FANCY DRAWN-WORK DOILY.

No. 48.—FINGER-BOWL DOILY IN DRAWN-WORK.

may desire, and no two patterns are alike. Single doilies are very pretty to place over satin toilet cushions; and whole sets for dressing a bureau or toilet table may be obtained to match, in any shape preferred.

BORDER IN DRAWN-WORK.

No. 49.—To make this border, draw threads from a space an inch and three-quarters wide, and either hem or knot-stitch the edges. Place the work wrong side up on an embroidery-hoop. With a straight thread carried through the middle, tie the threads into bunches of eighteen threads each. Tie in the side threads. With the last thread, weave in the spider in the center and make a web once around it. Make smaller spiders where the web-threads cross each other.

There is a wavy effect in this work that is exquisite and is especially pretty when the material is pongee—a fabric often used for scarfs or throws, in cream-white or écru. Several rows of the design and one row

are left after the drawing, and which form the foundation of the work.

FINGER-BOWL DOILY IN DRAWN-WORK.

No. 48.—No adequate degree of the delicacy of the doily represented can be conveyed by the engraving. The latter shows the design and the style of the article; but when the real doily is laid upon the hand one wonders how such a dainty result could be attained with nothing to assist the eye and the fingers. The work is developed upon a square of lawn, and when cut out a fine picot border is

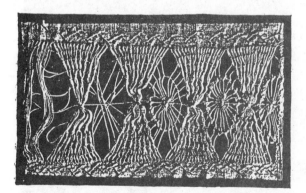

No. 49.—BORDER IN DRAWN-WORK.

worked about the edge. This renders the work firm and renovation possible. Finger-bowl doilies like the one here illustrated, as well as larger doilies are sold by the dozen or singly as the customer

of fringe may be used upon one end of a throw, and fringe alone upon the other end.

RUFFLE OF DRAWN-WORK AND LAWN.

No. 50.—This illustration shows a dainty strip of lawn decorated with drawn-work. The drawn-work at the top of the engraving is intended for insertion to be set above the gathered edge of the ruffle, and that at the bottom is above a hem which is to be at the edge of the ruffle when it is gathered.

No. 50.—RUFFLE OF DRAWN-WORK AND LAWN.

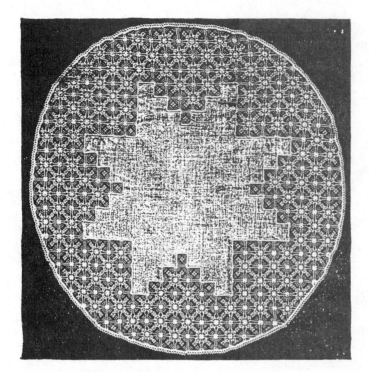

NO. 51.—ROUND DOILY OF DRAWN-WORK.

DRAWN-WORK DOILY.

(For Illustration see Page 95.)

No. 53.—This unique doily requires a piece of either French embroidery-linen or fine brown linen, nine inches square. One inch from each edge draw threads for the heading of the fringe, and hemstitch the space. One quarter of an inch from the fringe draw a thread each way, stopping it a quarter of an inch from each edge. Begin at the corner and measure two inches each way on the threads last drawn. ·Draw a thread each way on this line as far as the other two were drawn. This will give a large and a small square and two oblongs. Cut the ends of the oblongs three threads away from the small square, and also at the opposite ends a quarter of an inch from the fringe. Button-hole the cut edges, draw the threads, and put the work in an embroidery hoop, with the wrong side up. Knot-stitch the sides, using eight threads for each knotting. Knot

ROUND DOILY OF DRAWN-WORK.

No. 51.—A new departure in drawn-work doilies is here illustrated. The round drawn-work doily is beautiful to look at but difficult to make, and is therefore more expensive than doilies of the ordinary shape. The one illustrated is exquisite in workmanship and the materials are very delicate ; yet the result is a unique doily that will last a lifetime in the hands of a careful owner.

DRAWN-WORK DOILY.

No. 52.—The doily here illustrated, like many others in this pamphlet, is of Mexican manufacture. Mexicans are artists in this kind of work and the poorer classes depend largely upon it for their maintenance. The engraving fully discloses the design which any expert can easily copy. Before an amateur undertakes the work it would be better for her to master the designs and details given in the earlier preceding pages of this pamphlet; she will then be fully equipped for undertaking elaborate designs.

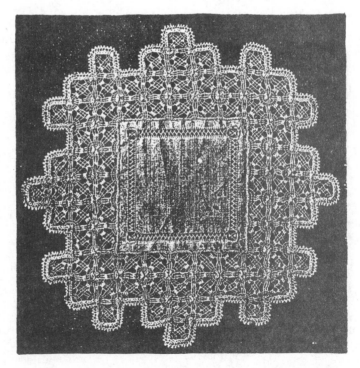

NO. 52.—DRAWN-WORK DOILY.

the rows below also, taking up eight bunches of threads each time. When putting in the other

No. 53.—DRAWN-WORK DOILY.

(For Description see Page 94.)

DRAWN-WORK DOILY.

No. 54.—This pretty doily may be very easily copied from the engraving without any special instructions. The threads are drawn to form open squares divided by bands of cross-threads, and small solid squares. Knottings and crossings of threads are then made as seen in the picture, and large and small spiders are formed around the knottings in the drawn spaces. The edges along the open spaces are button-holed, and a band of the fabric, feather-stitched, is left to form a heading for the fringe, which results from drawning threads of the fabric for about an inch at each side.

Very sheer linen lawn may be used for such doilies; and the same design may be extended over a larger space to form squares for tables or rose-jars, or for any other similar purpose.

Not infrequently doilies of this description are made with a tiny hem which in turn is bordered

threads do not tie where they cross, excepting in the third spaces. The spider webs are made with the last thread put in. Cut out the square in the corner on the threads drawn on the two outer edges, and three threads inside the threads drawn on the two inner sides. Button-hole all around. The cross-threads are all put in first. Then the thread must be broken and tied in the middle of each spider. Finish the work with a row of feather-stitching all around the doily, and one row around the plain square. An initial may be worked on the plain square. This pattern is very suitable for tray-cloths or center-pieces, or for a runner for a dinner-table.

In some doilies of this variety a row of satin ribbon is laid under the drawn-work; or if the fabric is very sheer the whole doily might be underlaid with tinted satin or silk. The plain center may also be decorated with hand-painting or embroidery. A pretty initial or monogram is a very popular centre for doilies of this kind.

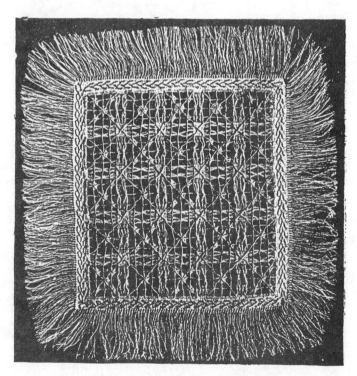

No. 54.—DRAWN-WORK DOILY.

with a frill of fine torchon or Valenciennes lace. The frill-effect is very attractive.

JAPANESE DRAWN-WORK DOILY.

No. 55.—This doily is made of Japanese silk or pongee of a delicate écru tint. It is about five inches square, but may be made as much larger as desired. The engraving represents it in a size pretty for finger-bowl or tumbler doilies. After the threads are drawn in the manner indicated, they may be knotted in any design preferred. Upon preceding pages of this pamphlet are numberless pretty designs, given in full size, and with explicit instructions for their development. Any of these designs could be adapted to Japanese doilies. Japanese silk could also be used for a handkerchief and the corners could be decorated with drawn-work the same as in articles made of linen.

No. 55.—JAPANESE DRAWN-WORK DOILY.

No. 56.—CORNER IN DRAWN-WORK.

CORNER IN DRAWN-WORK.

No. 56.—This design is for a corner two and a one-fourth inches square, but it can be used to good advantage as a continuous pattern. Divide the space into three sections each way, each section being three-fourths of an inch square. Cut the two outer edges at each corner space and draw the threads, first button-holing the cut edges. Hemstitch around the square in the center, making fourteen stitches on each side. Hemstitch the outer ends of the threads left after the other threads were drawn, taking care to take up the same threads for a stitch that were taken up around the center. Cut out the inside of the center square three threads from the outer edges. Button-hole the edges. Put the work wrong side up on an embroidery frame, and work the design as seen in the picture. The frame will hold the fabric taut and even, and the work will then be smooth when completed.

No. 57.—DRAWN-WORK DOILY.

DRAWN-WORK DOILY.

No. 57.—Large doilies like the one seen at No. 57 come in sets of six or twelve, with no two alike, or may be purchased singly, and are as dainty as the most fastidious housekeeper could desire. Sets containing tumbler, finger-bowl and plate doilies, center-pieces and mats may be ordered or purchased already made.

"MARGUERITE" DRAWN-WORK. (DETAIL.)

No. 58.—Draw out thirty threads, and leave twelve each way for as many squares as you require. (Four squares will repeat the Marguerite twice.)

Begin at the upper left-hand corner and knot the thread across the square four times. Pass the thread back to the border (upper left-hand corner of next lower square), and knot four threads across those you have already knotted, taking care to separate them as evenly as possible. Make all the foundation before begining the rest of the work.

To Make the Wheel.—Catch the thread into the linen at the back of the work at any center where the linen threads cross, and knot round very closely, taking three threads of linen to each knot; there will be thirty-two knots on the circle. Make the wheel with three rows of knots, or two widely separated. Make all the wheels before beginning the daisies.

To Make the Marguerite or Daisy.—Begin at next center and darn up two threads, till you have a sufficiently long leaf; then return the thread to the center at the back of the work and darn the next leaf.

The outer edge of the daisy may be darned last, or each leaf may be connected with the preceding one as you work. The daisy may be done more neatly by darning back to the center each time instead of passing the thread back.

Care should be taken to knot all the threads into the same hole in the center, to make a round eye for the daisy. Also draw the linen centers up closely so that your wheels may be round and even. Upon its regularity depends the beauty of the work.

No. 58.—"MARGUERITE" DRAWN-WORK. (DETAIL.)

CORNER OF DRAWN-WORK DOILY.

NOS. 59 AND 60.—The engraving at No. 59 represents a section of a very pretty doily of fine linen lawn. It should be about eleven inches square,

NO. 59.—CORNER OF DRAWN-WORK DOILY.

including the fringe, when finished. Cut the square from the lawn and about an inch in from its edge draw two or three threads each way to mark the depth of the fringe, and knot-hemstitch the threads that are left so that they will form strands, when the fringe is ravelled. Next draw the threads for the first border (see picture), knot-hemstitch the edges to form strands and arrange the latter as seen in the engraving, forming a star-shaped figure in the corner. Next draw threads for the broad border, leaving a cluster of threads through the middle of the section and cutting away threads crossing in the opposite direction to form open squares (see No. 60). Button-hole the edges of the border as seen in the engraving and then wrap the strands into fine ropes with the knotting cotton and also fill in the spaces and darn the figures as seen at No. 60. Then make the inner border, which is the same as the outer one, remove the work from the frame and ravel out the fringe.

TIDY OF SCRIM AND DRAWN-WORK, WITH DETAILS.

(For Illustration see Page 99.)

NOS. 61, 63 AND 64.—These illustrations show how simple patterns of drawn-work may be adapted to specimens of fancy work with very ornamental results.

No. 61 represents one corner of a tidy which is about sixteen inches square and is made of scrim, though silk, pongee or linen may be used for the same purpose. In this instance all of the knotting is made with orange-colored embroidery silk, and the narrow running ribbon matches in color. As the work and design are both exceedingly simple, and are but variations of details before given, it will not be necessary to give full instructions for following them. The accompanying engravings make the method perfectly clear even to a beginner.

It may be well, however, to mention the short upright stitch seen in every diamond or cross stitch along the heading of the tidy, and in the detail seen at No. 63. This is worked separately where the strands are not knotted, the loose end of the silk at figure No. 63 showing where the stitch passes through after being carried along at the back of the strand. Where strands are knotted (see No. 61), the knotting thread is also used for the short stitch by being passed upward back of the work after a knot

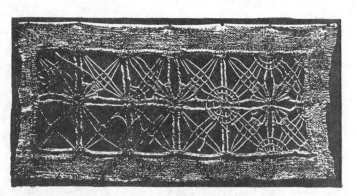

NO. 60.—DETAIL OF DRAWN-WORK DOILY.

is made, then over the top between the cross-stitches, through the fabric and down the back to the next strand for the next knot. This heading may be varied in any artistic manner to please the worker.

or any previous pattern or design may be substituted for it.

At No. 64 the method of making the fringe and its heading is illustrated. Each row is drawn and knotted independently of the other rows, care being

The ribbon is No. 1 width, and is satin with a straight edge. The cord is made of four threads of the embroidery silk doubled and twisted, and it is coiled to correspond with the wheels and has loops of a graceful length. The tassels are made

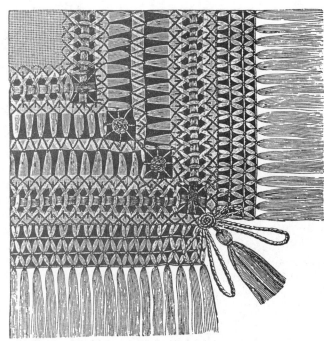

No. 61.—TIDY OF SCRIM AND DRAWN-WORK.

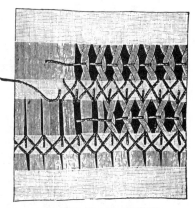

No. 63.—DETAIL OF TIDY.

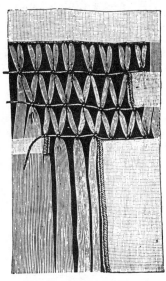

No. 64.—DETAIL OF TIDY.
(For Descriptions of Figures Nos. 61, 63 and 64, see Pages 98 and 99.)

observed to have the strands follow the arrangement seen ; and where only a portion of the work is to be drawn at a time, the raw edges should be protected by the button-hole stitches seen in the picture. After the lower or last knotting is made, the cross-threads are drawn to free the fringe ; and

No. 62.—DESIGN FOR DRAWN-WORK.

the heading to the latter may be as deep or as narrow as liked. The wheels at the corners are made by weaving the silk over and under the radiating threads or spokes.

of the ravellings of the scrim and a few strands of the silk.

DESIGN FOR DRAWN-WORK.

No. 62.—Draw three rows of thirty threads each, leaving six threads between each row. Cut and draw rows of nine cross-threads, leaving four threads after drawing each until across the work. The cross-threads are caught in the middle and tied very closely, as seen in the picture. Then whip the edges very closely and draw the horizontal thread across the middle of the spaces ; then add the diagonal ones until every other hexagon forms a star having twelve threads crossing the center. The design may be as many rows deep as desired.

CHAPTER XXIII.

SPECIMENS OF SPANISH, MEXICAN, DANISH, BULGARIAN, AND MODERN DRAWN-WORK.

END OF BUREAU SCARF IN DRAWN-WORK.

No. 1.

Upon the opposite page and a following one are illustrated the two ends of a very elaborate bureau scarf, which is made of embossed linen and decorated with drawn-work.

By a close inspection of No. 1, five distinct varieties of drawn-work will be seen, either of which by itself, will form a handsome decoration as a border. Combined, their beauty is beyond question. As each portion is separated from the adjoining one by a narrow band of the material left while drawing the threads, it will be seen that the work of combination will not be at all difficult. Each little intervening band is over-wrought with feather stitching, while the band between the lower border and the fringe has a fanciful decoration of feather stitching and embroidered dots. At least three of the designs are perfectly familiar to the eye of the student, to whom any slight deviation in detail will not matter, so long as it may easily be followed.

Frequently this design, or a similar combination of designs will be seen with the knotting made of unbleached cotton or linen, or of white or tinted silk, and in this event an intermingling of whichever is used, will appear in the fringe, being fastened into the fabric before the knotting of the fringe strands is made.

This scarf should be the full width of the linen—about twenty-two inches—and a yard and a-half or three-quarters long. The fringe is almost eight inches deep and is shown in full size and width on another page.

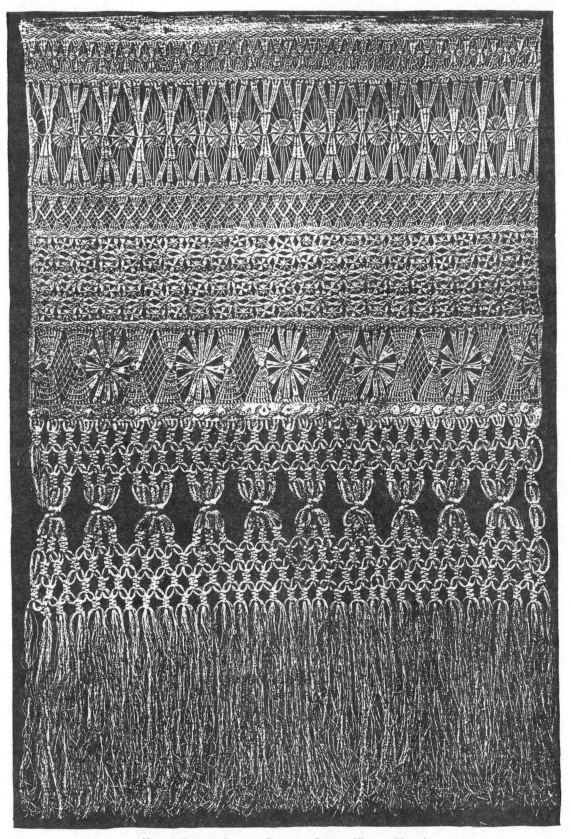

No. 1.—END OF BUREAU SCARF IN DRAWN-WORK. (No. 1.)

SECTION OF A SQUARE IN DRAWN-WORK.

No. 2.

A section of a very showy square which may be used for many purposes of a decorative nature is here illustrated. The article itself is about thirteen inches across from side to side, and is made of heavy linen and quite coarse knotting cotton. The texture of the fabric, the size of the cotton and the character of the design, all tend to produce a rich and effective piece of work that would, naturally, developed in conjunction with sheer linen and fine cotton, result in a square of dainty beauty similar in effect to the delicate Mexican or Spanish drawn-work.

In preceding portions of this book will be found knottings and darnings similar to those seen in this engraving, so that special instructions will not be needed for this particular design by any one who has followed the previous directions named, or who will refer to them now. The only peculiarity of the design is the formation of the rings around the fans, and this is very easily done. When all the strands have been knotted, and the fans tied at the middle, then a single knotting thread is carried around each fan and across the intervening threads, and is knotted to each strand and thread to hold it firmly in place. Then over this single thread are closely-made button-hole stitches so arranged as to form a raised ring with their edges. A very pretty effect is obtained by using silk for these rings and the stars, and cotton only for knotting the strands. A square like the one illustrated should be laid over a lining of colored silk, also fringed, and is very pretty to use under vases, lamps, rose jars, bric-a-brac, etc., etc.

No. 2.—Section of a Square in Drawn-Work.

TRAY CLOTH OF LINEN AND DRAWN-WORK.

No. 3.

This tray cloth, a corner of which and one side are here represented, is made of fine butcher's linen, and is thirty inches long by twenty-two inches wide. The engraving shows it of about half size, so that in making it, the fringe, imitation hem and drawn-work should be about twice as wide as here seen.

In making it, if preferred, the edge may have a real hem, which may be made and fringed out by the instructions given for No. 1, on page 62.

The design for the drawn-work is exceedingly pretty and effective, and at the same time very easy to make. The open spaces are filled in by crossing threads of the knotting cotton, and then a spider's web is made by methods heretofore illustrated and explained, and which are here also made perfectly plain by the engraving. The crosses seen upon the solid squares are made as follows : At each side, between the strands, fasten knotting threads, crossing them at the center of the square and fastening them at that point by a knot taken through the fabric. Then darn over and under each set of threads as seen in the picture, beginning at the knot and carrying the thread, when the section is darned, down under the darning to the knot again, in order to begin another section. This fastens the cross down at the center of the fabric only, and leaves it like raised embroidery upon the block.

The cloth represented is knotted throughout with cotton, but a very elaborate effect may be produced by using silk for darning the centers of the webs and the crosses, and making the little round spots or rosettes between the strands. White silk is preferable, as it washes better than colored silk, though the latter, in wash silks, is considerably used for such work.

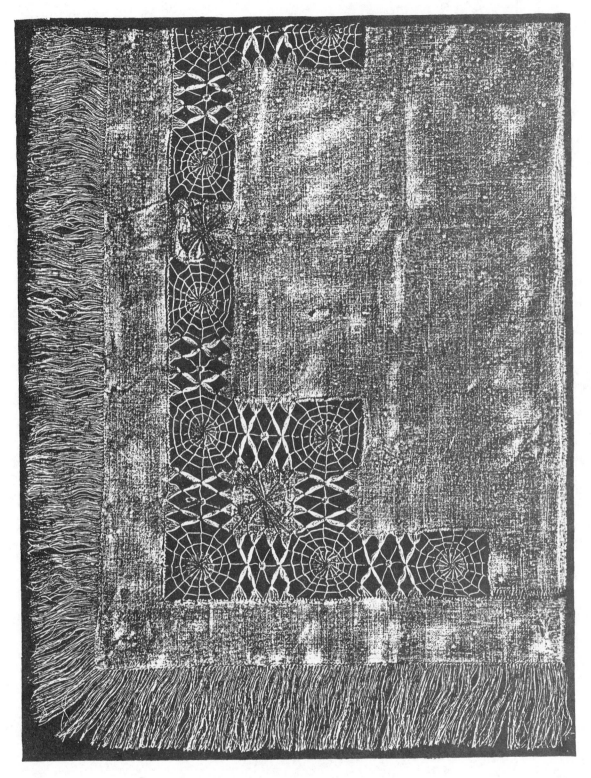

NO. 3.—TRAY CLOTH OF LINEN AND DRAWN-WORK.

DETAILS FOR DECORATING BUREAU–SCARF END.

No. 4.

Upon page 101 is shown a handsomely decorated scarf end ; but though a good general effect was obtained, the details are not delineated plainly enough to be accurately followed. In this engraving they are repeated on a larger scale and may be easily copied.

The extreme upper border is knotted in a novel design, which, though showy is very simply done. Fans of four strands each are knotted through their centers and then by two other knotting cottons, the last one of which is darned over and under the crossed cottons to form the rosette seen. After this the alternate upper and lower halves of the fans are darned as seen in the picture.

In the wide row below, nine strands are first tied through the center for each fan, the knotting thread being continuous. Then two other threads at each side are knotted along the fans as in the upper row. When this is done the solid darning is made, and then each three strands above it are darned as seen in the picture, the ends of the outer darnings being brought down to the center of the crossed threads ; then other threads are added until there are twenty spokes for each rosette, and the latter is darned round and round by the point d'angleterre lace stitch—a stitch illustrated and described in our book on Lace-Making, and also on other pages of this book.

The method for the next band is fully described in chapter XIII., while the next lower band may be formed upon the principles found in chapter X.

The remaining band may easily be worked by an inspection of the engraving, and by previous instructions found in various parts of the book.

No. 4.—Details for Decorating Bureau-Scarf End.

SPECIMEN OF DANISH DRAWN-WORK.

No. 5.

This engraving represents a specimen of Danish drawn-work, which is easy to make and showy in effect, as it introduces considerable embroidery done in satin-stitch. The sample may easily be copied by the eye and needs no detailed instructions. Use embroidery silk for the knotting and satin-stitch. The latter is nearly alike on both sides, and is a species of over-and-over stitch. The fabrics employed for Danish drawn-work are canvas, scrim and bolting-cloth.

A pretty square of Danish drawn-work was about half-a-yard across, and was made of fine white canvas and white embroidery silk. The design was similar to the one here illustrated, except that considerable open-work was displayed along the diagonal portions of the design.

This was made by cutting the threads in the customary way, and securing the edges of the openings by button-hole or over-and-over stitches done in very fine cotton and then covered with the silk thread. The square was hemmed by a fancy hemstitch; and two oblong sections, made to match, formed the set which was for a bureau.

As canvas fringes prettily, a hem might be simulated above a border of fringes the same as in the tray cloth seen at No. 3, on page 105; but as a rule articles decorated with Danish drawn-work are finished with hems.

No. 5.—Specimen of Danish Drawn-Work.

SECTION OF DOILY IN SPANISH DRAWN-WORK.

No. 6.

A section of a doily, full size, of Spanish drawn-work is here represented. The example was square, but the design may be applied to oblong doilies of any size desired. The object in giving a full-size representation is to make the details so apparent that no instruction will be needed by students who have mastered the previous designs of the book in developing the design; and the engraver has succeeded perfectly in giving a faithful reproduction of the work.

A reference to No. 7, chapter IX., however, may assist the worker in completing the border; and an inspection of No. 18, on page 77, will show her exactly how each knotting thread is taken through every little solid square of the fabric, though this detail is very plainly depicted here.

The darnings are very easy to follow, and when completed, have a Maltese-cross effect that is very attractive. When this doily is made of silk, all the darning and knotting should be done with embroidery silk either in white or tints or a commingling of the two. Embroidery silk may also be used in connection with cotton or linen thread in making a doily of linen lawn; but if the fabric is quite sheer, it is better to use use cotton alone as the effect is then very delicate and fairy-like. Such doilies may be used upon the toilet table or under finger bowls, punch glasses, rose jars, vases, etc., etc.

No. 6.—Section of Doily in Spanish Drawn-Work.

END OF BUREAU SCARF IN DRAWN-WORK.

No. 7.

The remaining end of the scarf, one end of which is pictured on page 101 and described on page 100, is here illustrated. While it does not present as many varieties in design as the end seen on the page mentioned it is excedingly effective, combining, as it does, features of Mexican, Spanish, Bulgarian and Danish drawn-work in its development. The rosettes appearing in the alternate spaces are pretty contrasts to the stars in the remaining spaces, though both are done by darning processes. A scarf-end in this design, the material selected being silk and the knotting threads also of silk, would form a rich drapery for a mantel, an upright piano, an easel, a mirror or any of the many pieces of furniture now stylishly draped with scarfs of all kinds. Done on heavy écru or colored canvas with coarse cotton or very fine fancy twine, this design, with its fringe, could be used in making a valance for a couch or for the edge of a mantel or a bracket. In making a long drapery of silk or linen, use the fabric with the selvedges at the top and bottom unless it is especially desired that the fabric be used lengthwise. In the latter event, instructions for neatly and properly joining the breadths will be found at No. 3. in chapter X.

The design may be used above plain fringe or a hem and tucks, or above a lace-trimmed hem if preferred. On pages 119 and 125 the fringe for both ends of the scarf will be given in full size so that either may be knotted with no difficulty.

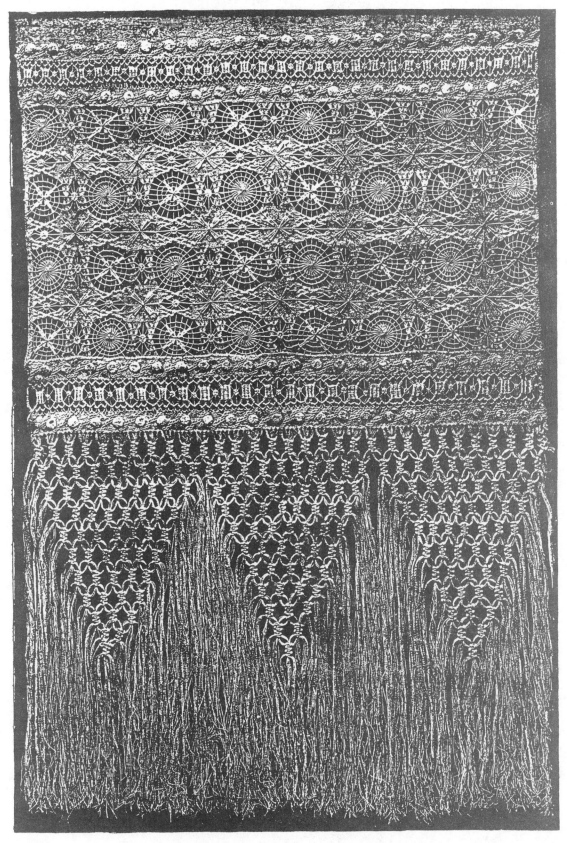

No. 7.—End of Bureau Scarf in Drawn-Work. (No. 2.)

DESIGN FOR A BUREAU SCARF.

No. 8.

The scarf from which this engraving was copied was made of linen of the weave illustrated, and was about sixty inches long and seventeen wide. A very pretty design was stamped upon it, between the ends, to be embroidered in outline stitch in colored wash-embroidery silks.

The drawn-work portion is here given of full size, so that no difficulty will be experienced in following it or in knotting the fringe. All of the knotting is simply done, but the result is extremely effective.

This design could be applied to towels, and without the fringe, to various articles of household use. If desired the knotting could be done with red or blue cotton or linen, and threads of the same could be incorporated with the fringe by knotting them into the fabric.

In other parts of the book will be found many designs which, or portions of which, could be applied to a fringed scarf or towel, or to any of the other articles suggested as appropriate for similar decorations. This engraving will afford a good idea as to how their application might or should be made.

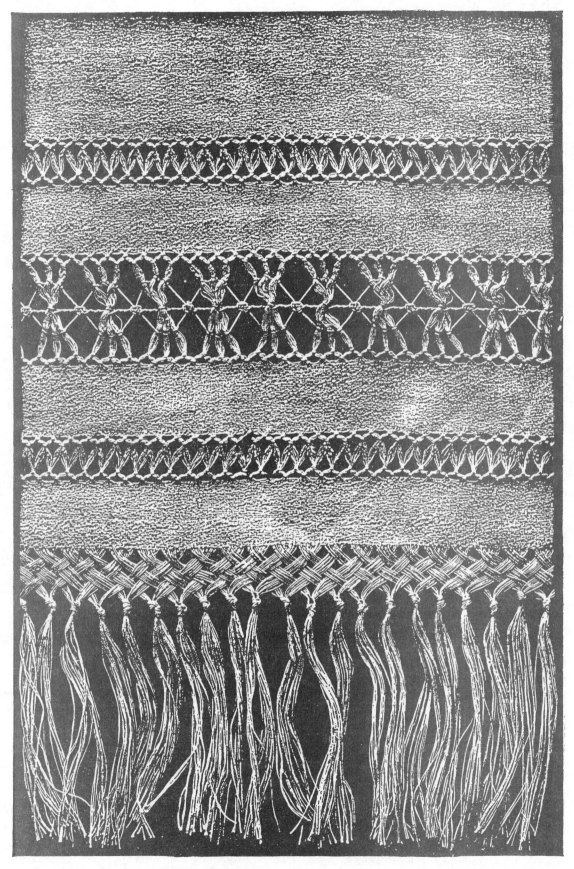

No. 8.—Design for a Bureau Scarf.

DOILY OF BULGARIAN DRAWN-WORK AND EMBROIDERY.

No. 9.

The specimen of drawn-work and embroidery here illustrated was made in Constantinople, and represents one variety of the many kinds done by women who were made refugees by the Russo-Turkish war, and who, losing all their possessions, flocked to the Turkish capital. Here, after a time, the "Turkish Compassionate Fund" was established by charitable English residents who saw in the many wonderful varieties of embroideries made by these unfortunate people, a source of maintenance for them. Materials were purchased, work was given out to the eager applicants, and from their specimen-productions grew up a great demand for the so-called Bulgarian work. Over two thousand needle-women are now employed by the society in supplying the most wonderful embroideries of the times.

The engraving represents a doily made of *pani*, a native material which is not unlike scrim in texture and color. All of the open-work is made by drawing the threads and then darning over and under the strands after the method described in chapter VI., except that in this instance only two strands at a time are darned together. The darning is done with cream-colored silk, which is also used for the star at the center of the doily, but the dark-tinted embroidery is done with fine gold thread. The beauty of the work is that it is exactly alike on both sides. The edge of the doily is daintily rolled and finished with a feathery-looking edge done with a needle and the silk thread.

The design will form a pretty one for doilies made of linen lawn or any sheer fabrics for which silk in white or tints is to be selected for the knotting, darning and embroidery. A native Eastern fabric much used is Broussa silk gauze, which resembles very fine silk bolting cloth; but aside from this gauze and *pani*, French fabrics are used exclusively for Bulgarian needle-work.

No. 9.—Doily of Bulgarian Drawn-Work and Embroidery.

SECTION OF FRINGE FOR A SCARF END.

No. 10.

This elaborate looking fringe is not difficult to make, especially if one is acquainted with the methods of tying macramé fringe, as one of the knottings employed for the latter was used in this case.

When the fringe has been knotted into strands by the method described in previous chapters, ravel out the remaining portion of the fabric and brush the fringe smoothly in place. Then knot it in rows as follows: Take four strands; hold the middle two firmly and loop the other two around them alternately after the macramé style, interweaving them so that they will not slip. A little practice with bits of cord will soon make the process clear to the student. Knot these outer strands, each *twice* around the middle strands of each group. Repeat across the end. For the next row take *two* of *each four* strands *before* used (see engraving) and proceed as before. For the next row the original four will be used for each knotting, and for the next row the *second* set of four will again be used. Then three sets of knottings will be looped together to form the heavy knotting as seen in the engraving; and the latter will also explain the progress of the remainder of the knotting.

As the fringe is about eight inches deep, considerably more than that in depth will have to be allowed before the knotting is begun, as the latter will take up some of the strands leaving them shorter than the others, and the fringe will thus have to be "evened off" with the shears when completed.

No. 10.—Section of Fringe for a Scarf End.

DETAILS FOR SCARF END.

No. 11.

As explained upon a preceding page, this design, without being particularly elaborate, is very effective. The clearness of the engraving will render the work perfectly intelligible.

The headings are alike and the method of their development may be found in chapters VI., IX. and X. where parts of the method are illustrated separately and described in the same manner. The decoration at each side of the headings has been mentioned on a recent page as a combination of feather-stitch and satin-stitch, and the engraving pictures it perfectly.

The main portion of the design is prepared in the usual manner by drawing threads to leave squares and spaces of equal dimensions. The intervening strands are knotted each way with fine cottons after the manner illustrated, after which vertical, horizontal and diagonal cottons cross the solid squares and open spaces, the last cotton of each direction named knotting all the other threads together at the centers of the spaces and blocks and being used to make the circular darnings. Other threads are added to the solid squares for the star-spokes as will be seen by referring to the engraving, but they pass through the fabric only, and do not cross the knottings. The stars on the solid squares are darned like those seen at No. 3 on page 105; while those in the circles, all of which have two or three extra knottings around them, are darned after the general method. The large rosettes are made by the point d'angleterre method, which carries the darning thread around each spoke before it passes on to the next one. This produces a ribbed effect which is very pretty. Like the other details, these may be applied to an infinite variety of articles for both household and personal wear.

No. 11.—Detail for Scarf End.

SQUARE OF MEXICAN DRAWN-WORK FOR A POT-POURRI OR ROSE JAR.

No. 12.

Although this square, a corner of which is represented by the engraving, is intended for placing under a *pot-pourri*, it may be used for any other similar purpose desired, according to the fabric from which it is made.

The section given is of full size, and the work is so clearly illustrated that little or no instruction will be necessary in following the design. The hem is made in the usual manner by the "Second Method" given in chapter II.; and the knotting of the narrow borders is done similarly to that seen at No. 2, in chapter IV., except that the knotting thread confines three strands at a time and extends along the middle of the row.

In preparing the wide border, but few strands of the fabric, which is fine linen, are left, and the spaces between them are quite large. Fine knotting cotton is used to tie the strands and fill in the spaces; and the method employed is made perfectly clear by the engraving, which shows distinctly every knot and crossing. On page 79, the detail for No. 21 will assist in forming the knottings at the middle of the spaces and the corners, while No. 18 on page 77 will make perfectly clear the looped stitches at the center of the solid blocks. Made of heavy linen this design would be very handsome for a tray cloth, table square, or a buffet or bureau scarf. In fine linen lawn it would be very dainty for handkerchiefs or toilet doilies; while in silk, pongee or silk bolting cloth it would prove very ornamental for tidies, drapery scarfs, etc., etc.

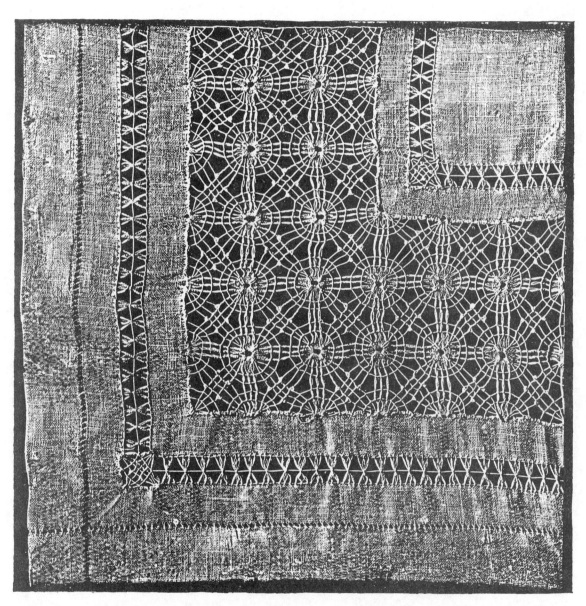

No. 12.—Square of Mexican Drawn-Work for a Pot-Pourri or Rose Jar.

FRINGE FOR SCARF END IN DRAWN-WORK.

No. 13.

The fringe here illustrated may again be seen as a finish for the scarf end shown by No. 7 on page 113. It is knotted upon the same plan as that described for the fringe seen upon page 119, and again appearing below the scarf end represented at No. 1 on page 101. The student of drawn-work will find great pleasure in inventing variations in knotting fringes, either after the method here given or by any of the many others seen in fancy-work books for the making of fringes. If, however, she does not care to knot the fringe, or does not find it an easy matter, she may let it fall in flowing strands from the knotting which confines the fringe at the top. Linen or silk always makes pretty fringe even if the fancy knotting is omitted.

An attractive method for finishing fringe is shown at No. 8, on page 115; and in a deeper fringe, the plaited effect could be extended considerably. In chapter VI. another effective method of knotting fringe is illustrated; and the method permits of the introduction of colored cotton or knotting thread into the heading of the fringe as well as the strands. In thin fabrics, where a deep fringe is desired, the plan adopted for the corner illustrated at No. 1 in chapter XX. may be made available with satisfactory results. Still another method of completing fringe will be found on page 99 with its description.

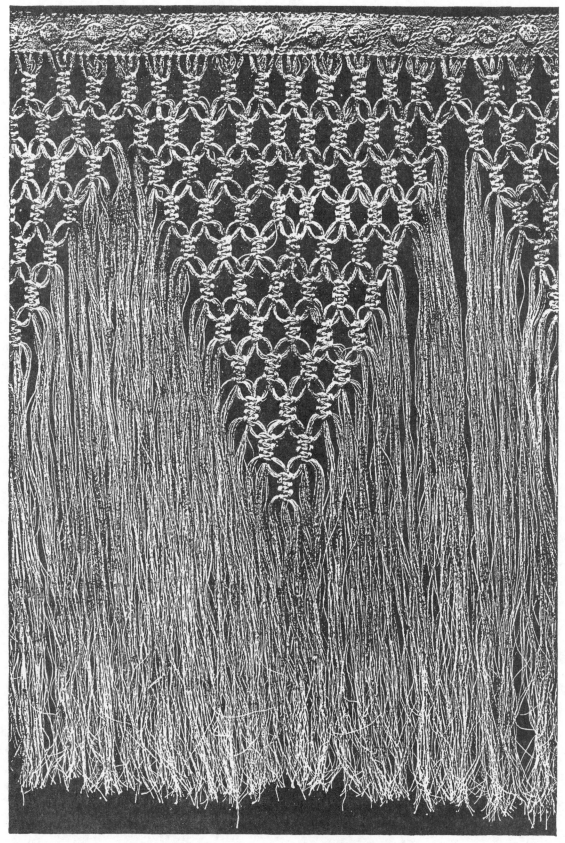

NO. 13.—FRINGE FOR SCARF END IN DRAWN-WORK.

DESIGN FOR A TOWEL BORDER IN DRAWN-WORK.

No. 14.

The design represented by this illustration is exceedingly easy to follow, and at the same time is very effective. The knot chain is used for the hemstitching effects, all of which have been frequently illustrated upon the preceding pages of this book and are therefore perfectly familiar. The wide border combines the details of one or two of the various designs heretofore given, and, if desired, may be used alone above the fringe or in connection with only one of the hemstitching effects. Plain linen of heavy weight makes very handsome towels as its threads are well adapted to drawn-work; but not infrequently fancy linen is chosen when drawn-work is to be the decoration used.

Usually all white is used in making decorated towels; but occasionally the knotting thread will be of the unbleached variety or of colored linen or cotton. This point must be submitted to personal taste, since it is a matter subject to no arbitrary rules or decisions.

The design under discussion, or portions of it may be applied to sheets, pillow cases, sheet and pillow shams, scarfs, tray cloths, table cloths or any article of household linen that may be appropriately decorated by drawn-work of a kindred variety.

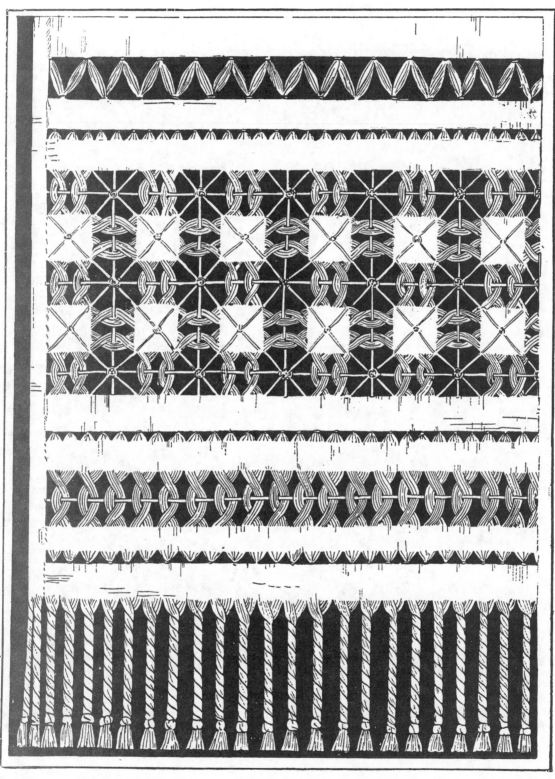

No. 14.—Design for a Towel Border in Drawn-Work.

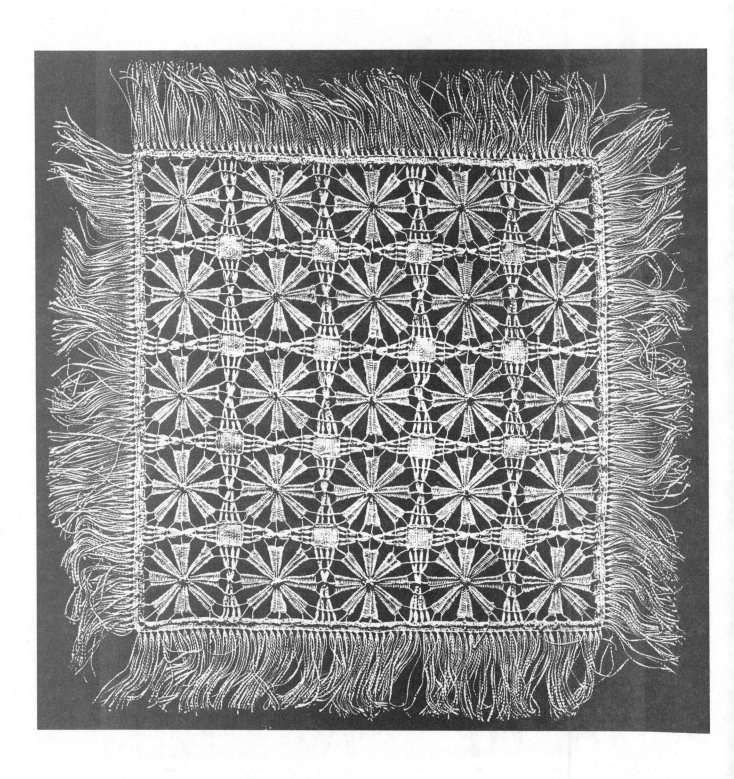